Inspired Artistry

Embracing the Creative Calling

A Southern Sky Devotional

Pamela Poole

Inspired Southern Ambiance

Published by
Southern Sky Publishing

Southern Sky Publishing southernskypublishing.com

Technical advisor: Andy Poole
All scripture references are from the Holman Christian Study Bible (HCSB), Holman Bible Publishers, USA
eBook ISBN 978-1-956089-09-7
Print ISBN 978-1-956089-10-3
KDP Print ISBN 979-8632335-99-7

Author's Notes

It is with a trembling hand that I write this devotional. Is *anyone* worthy of relating Christ's mind about anything? Only those who rely on Scripture, yet even then, we may fall short by interpreting it through our own baggage of experiences, religious traditions, prejudices, and agendas.

Those who earnestly seek His mind and heart will always grow in wisdom until the day they pass from this life and enter Heaven. The Bible is a living book the Holy Spirit uses to delve deeper into my heart, mind, and soul. For that reason, I will know more of my Creator the day after this devotional is published than the days when I wrote it. If your understanding of living a creative calling as a Christian is higher than the words you read here in my little devotional, I hope to find grace in your eyes while I travel my unique road toward having the mind of Christ, my Creator and Redeemer.

How to Use This Book

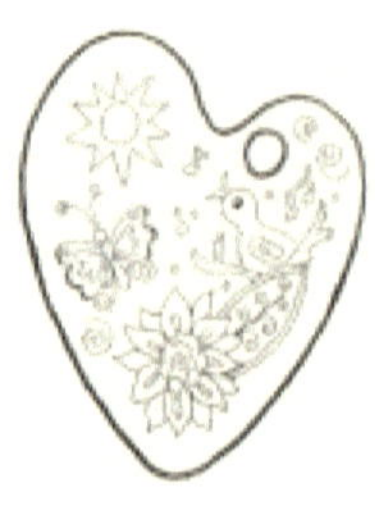
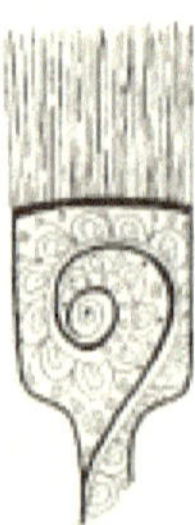
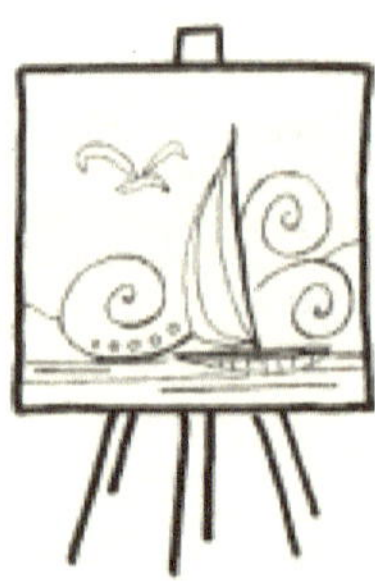

AS FRIENDS LEARNED that I was writing a Christian devotional book, they let me know they wanted something different from the predictable constraints of the usual format in devotionals. So, rather than the typical drive-through presentation of 150 words, *Inspired Artistry* is arranged in twelve chapters of about 1,200 words. Readers can study and pray about the chapter contents over several days.

I humbly suggest that if you are enjoying the book, journal through the material. If you have the print copy, there are blank pages at the end titled "Inspired Musings" for noting verses, thoughts, and pages to find later. You may also feel inspired to use the illustrations as coloring pages, embellishing them in your style with your favorite art supplies. Look for free downloads of the illustrations on my websites. If you or your kids color the pages and post a photo on social media, I'd be honored if you'd tag me so I can enjoy them, too!

My personal insights and interpretations in this devotional may be new views for you on a topic. Look up the scripture references in a study Bible and compare them to others online. At the end of each chapter is a section to solidify the intended message in the theme.

Another unique departure in this book from a typical devotional is that I refer to my points in art terms–as if readers are working on their masterpiece. I've created original icons that will appear before information for that theme. They are a **Palette, Brush,** and painting on an easel called the **Big Picture**.

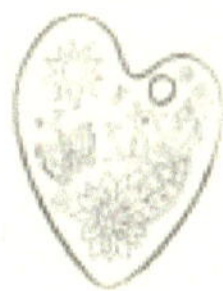

A **Palette** is an invaluable tool by which artists arrange the paint they will use in their pictures. People who collect and study the palettes of various artists in history learn a lot about an artist's personality and style, and invariably, the dried paint smears on the palette match the favorite range of colors in the artist's works. After careful thought and planning, an artist squeezes out paint he knows will give him the best chance of accomplishing his desired outcome, then he mixes a spectrum of nuanced colors. In this devotional, our Palette will feature universal truths and Scripture as the basis for foundational tools to work with for our Big Picture.

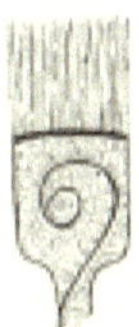

An artist's **Brush** is the tool he uses to link his Palette with his canvas. A typical art studio will have on hand an assortment of paintbrushes in many sizes and shapes. The artist will rely on experience, skills, head knowledge, and trial and error to apply brushstrokes of paint from his palette. In this devotional, our **Life Brush** is about our application of the truth on our Palette as we work toward our **Big Picture**.

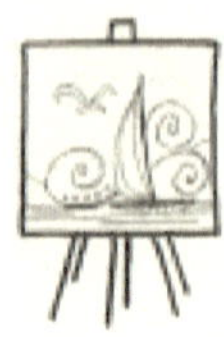

A FINISHED PAINTING is the goal of every artist when they start out with a Palette of paint and a loaded Brush. In this devotional, our **Big Picture** is the goal we strive for as we embrace a creative life—a life lived in the image of our Creator.

Stay tuned at the end of this book for an excerpt from Landmark, Painter Place Saga 4, to peek into the life of a Christian professional artist.

"I unconsciously decided that, even if it wasn't an ideal world, it should be so and painted only the ideal aspects of it."
Norman Rockwell

The Origin of the Creative Calling

"In the beginning God created the heavens and the earth."
Genesis 1:1

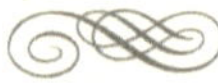

THE HOLY BIBLE OPENS with the first revelation about an attribute of God: He is creative.

Every time I come across lists and studies of the attributes of God, I'm awestruck. An "attribute" is a quality or feature regarded as a characteristic or inherent part of someone or something. In this devotional, we'll be focusing on God's creativity and how it is reflected in us.

Genesis Chapter 1, Psalm 33:6-9, and the opening verses of the Gospel of John tell us God spoke things into existence. Then in Genesis 2:7, He reveals something almost incomprehensible to me! With His own hands, he fashioned Adam after Himself—from the dust of the ground. The word used in the account is the same one used elsewhere in scripture for a potter. Next, He shared His own breath to ignite life within man, a transformation into a unique mix of spirit and the physical.

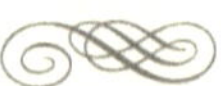

"The heavens were made by the word of the Lord,
and all the stars, by the breath of His mouth.
He gathers the waters of the sea into a heap;
He puts the depths into storehouses.
Let the whole earth tremble before the Lord;

let all the inhabitants of the world stand in awe of Him.
For He spoke, and it came into being;
He commanded, and it came into existence."
Psalm 33:6-9

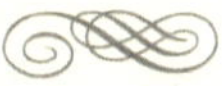

READING OVER TO GENESIS 2:18-20, we find that God issued the first recorded creative call. He brought each animal before Adam to see what he would call it. Animals did not receive God's breath during their creation, as man had, so Adam ruled over the animals and perceived their nature to give them appropriate names. Since none of the animals were on man's level, God fashioned a mate for him from the flesh and bone in his side. Once again, Adam had the creative calling to name her. The term he used, "woman," is the feminine complement to his own name, "man."

One of my favorite chapters of Scripture is Job 38. It reminds me that God's creative power is incomprehensible and purposeful. He's engaged with the world, watching over everything, and nothing is wasted.

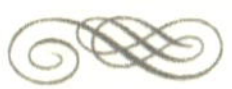

"Where were you when I established the earth?
Tell Me, if you have understanding.
Who fixed its dimensions? Certainly you know!
Who stretched a measuring line across it?
What supports its foundations?
Or who laid its cornerstone
while the morning stars sang together
and all the sons of God shouted for joy?"
Job 38: 4-11

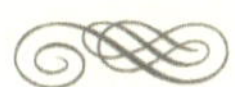

IF WE RECOGNIZE THE imprint of our Creator on our lives, we may come to consider our creative gifts as a *calling*. We allow Christ to work in unexpected ways with images, dreams, and experiences. He is intentional about inspiring us and gathering the threads woven into the tapestry of our lives.

Every person born into the world has been created in the image of God, stamped with attributes of their Maker even if they do not acknowledge Him. (John 1:9). Creativity is in our nature, and because we turned the perfect world that He gave us into a cursed one, mankind uses this trait for good or evil. This comes from having a choice, which is another attribute of God. In her book *The Mind of the Maker,* author Dorothy Sayers asserts her belief that when people feel at odds with their God-placed creativity, it's because a distortion makes them run counter to their nature.

The distortion Sayers referred to was clear in my research for this devotional. When I read quotes from art history by artists who attempted to define art or give people a glimpse of their intentions, it was evident that the powerful drive inside their souls mystified them. So many artists focused on themselves as the source for the outward expressions they shared with the world. Entangled in their fleeting, unstable feelings as their imaginations caught fire from stimulation in life, they believed self-expression was the goal of their work.

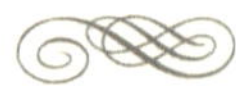

"God stepped from behind the curtain of nowhere and stood on the platform of nothing, then spoke a world into existence."
-unknown African American Pastor

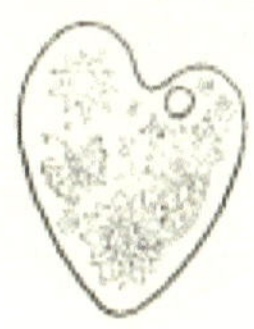

WE ARE CREATED IN GOD'S image, Genesis Chapters 1:26-2:22

We are to do everything as if we dedicated it to Christ, Colossians 3:23,24

We have a purpose and can trust Christ for outcomes, Colossians 1:16

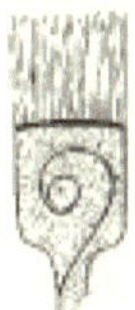

HAVE YOU EVER PRAYERFULLY asked Jesus to guide you along the best path for using the gifts, skills, and talents He has stamped on your soul?

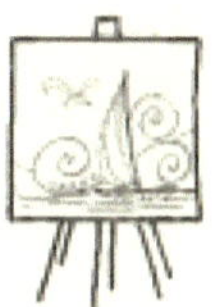

INSTEAD OF LIVING AS the world does, via their philosophy of being an accident in the universe through random processes, Christians live and create in the assurance of being lovingly made as Christ's handiwork, like a poem (Ephesians 2:10). We embrace His gifts, skills, and talents as we dedicate our efforts to Him and share as He leads.

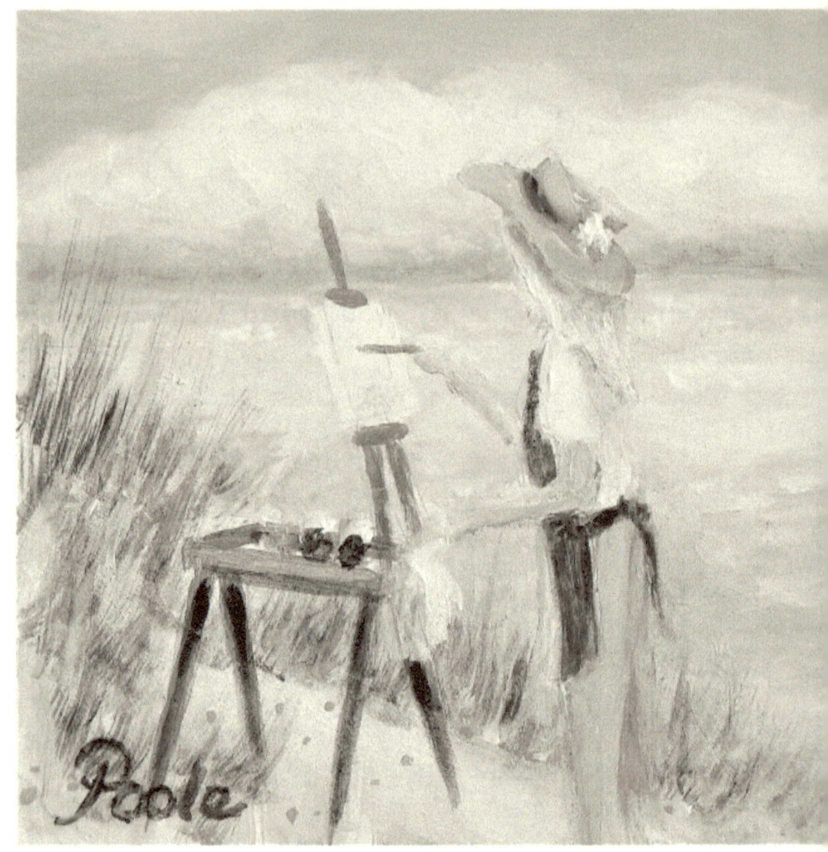

"Beach Studio"

A World We Close Our Eyes to See

"Whatever is born of the flesh is flesh, and whatever is born of the Spirit is spirit."
John 3:6

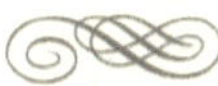

WHAT IS CREATIVITY, and why is it significant to mankind? Not even Scripture provides a satisfying description of the mystery of how the Holy Spirit moves us. In a passage that speaks to artistic gifting in designing and crafting the Israelite tabernacle in the wilderness, we are told, "He has filled them with skill to do all the work of a gem cutter; a designer; an embroiderer in blue, purple, and scarlet yarn and fine linen; and a weaver. They can do every kind of craft and design artistic designs." (Exodus 35:35).

One illustration about how some people apply the elusive gift of imagination is "The Greatest Showman," a recent movie based loosely on the life of P. T. Barnum. Barnum is credited with being the father of show-business. In the movie, Hugh Jackman sings the song "A Million Dreams." The lyrics speak of his constant creative vision about a world he closes his eyes to see. In another song called "Tightrope," the lyrics speak of the risk people take when they live their creative calling. Adventure and the breathtaking view from a higher place make the risk worth everything.

The remarkable theme of the tale is that the dreamers and visionaries of the world will enhance the lives of those who suppress creativity for security. Artistic vision is often relegated to the status of an elusive magic formula, and a creative spirit is considered unstable.

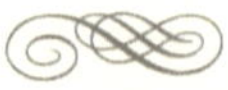

"The Christian is the one whose imagination should fly beyond the stars." Francis A. Shaeffer, *Art and the Bible*

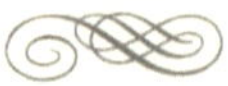

IN HER BOOK *The Mind of the Maker*, Dorothy Sayers writes that the mind of an artist is in a higher place than the world's thinking of judgements and practical solutions. She refers to this state of being as "living in the way of grace" and believes an artist's creative nature is unconscious as he pursues a mysterious way of life. He often works a day job for money to survive, but then escapes to find fulfillment for his spirit in the freedom *from* money.

Just as the Holy Spirit is enigmatic in the Bible, so is the spirit-led life of the creative Christian. In Genesis 1:2, we see the Spirit as an agent of creation with God, bringing order out of chaos. In Chapter 2:7, we see the Spirit moving as the invisible Breath of God to ignite life into man.

When we feel called or led to a project, we may begin with an idea of what we hope to accomplish. Then it takes on a life and direction of its own! A Christian artist becomes the servant being led by the Spirit of his/her Maker.

When this phenomenon happens to me, my heart leaps and overflows with sudden joy and recognition. I feel a momentary breathlessness. And as my mind grapples with the implications of obedience to the calling, I'm almost crippled with humility. Only my Savior can use my insignificance to be meaningful, whether for a work in me or in an audience He will bring to it. "Self-expression" doesn't occur to me. Indeed, it would ruin the work.

It would take another Bible Study to delve into the ways the Holy Spirit fills, moves, and works in the lives of believers. He is a Person, with intellect, (Romans 8:27), actions (John 8, 1 Corinthians 12), feelings (Ephesians 4:30), a will, and He doesn't come to our lives in stages, but all at once, the instant we receive Christ as our Savior. If we follow our calling of creativity, we are reflecting God's image to the world and bringing glory to Him. That's what the Holy Spirit within us does—He leaps at truth and testifies to the Gospel of Jesus Christ.

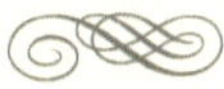

"The great God of the universe who heaped up the mountains, scooped out the oceans, and flung out the stars wants to have a relationship with you."

Adrian Rogers, American Pastor, 1931-2005

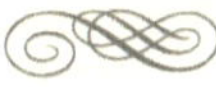

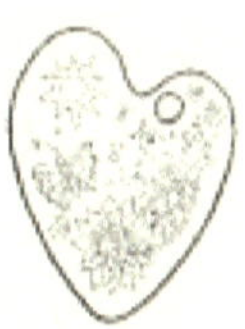

THE SPIRIT-LED LIFE of a Christian believer seems peculiar and strange because God's ways aren't man's ways. Artists, musicians, writers, and craftsmen are sometimes called dreamers for living out their creative calling because they are accepting the imprint of their Creator.

Exodus 35:35

1 Corinthians 3:16

2 Corinthians 3:17

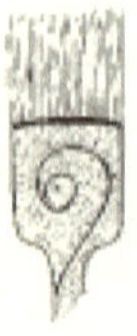

IF YOU DON'T ALREADY know what your creative calling is, pray for Jesus to make your gifts clear. Are you trying to control that giftedness within the confines of what is "normal" or are you're allowing the horses to run free?

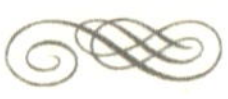

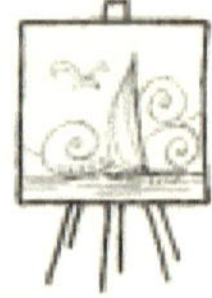

YOU ARE STAMPED WITH the image of your Creator. When you asked Him to be your Savior, you asked Him to take over your life. Your dreams gave way to His dreams for you, and they live outside your comfort zone.

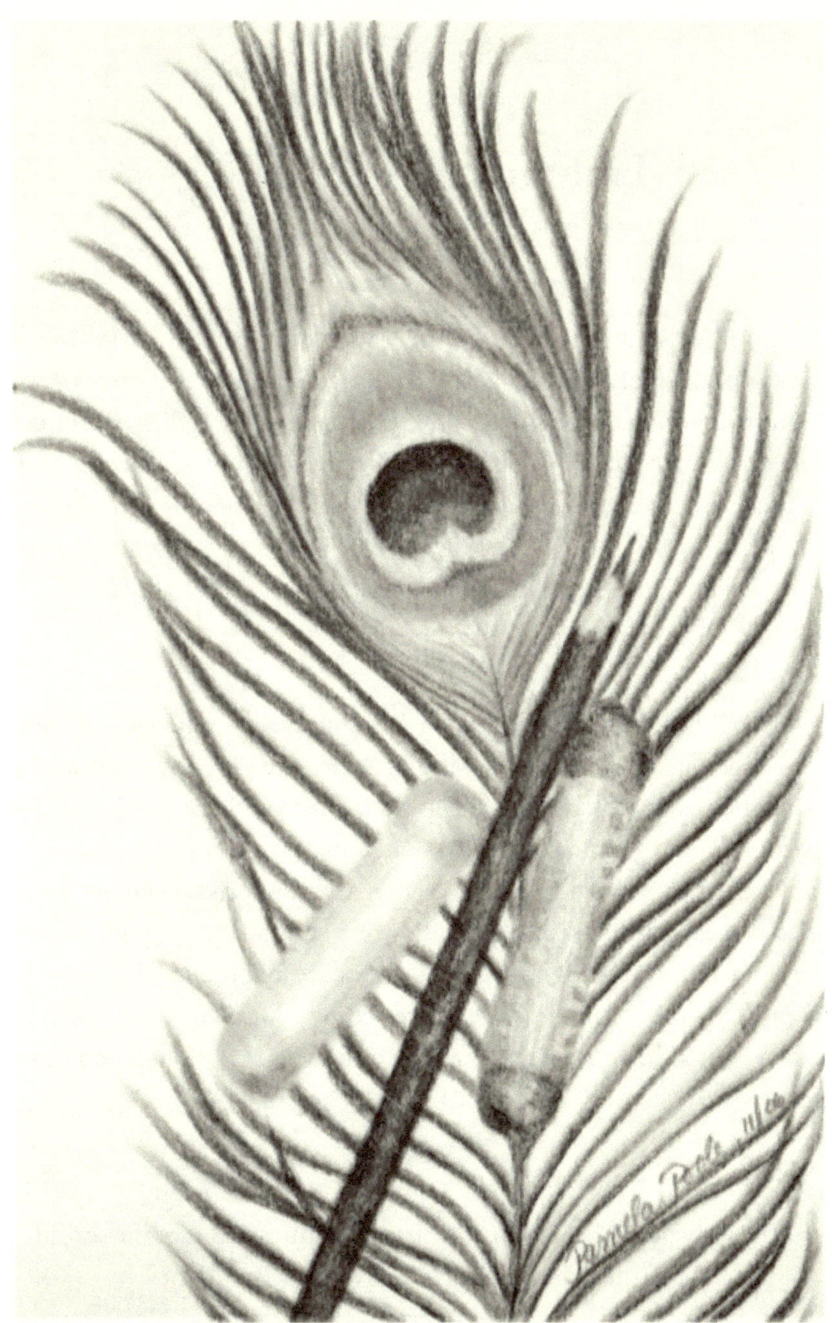

Embracing Your Calling

"Since Christians, artists as well as evangelists, have within them the power of the Holy Spirit, it is only logical to conclude that artists, who bring everything into captivity for Christ, write, just as they live, under the direction of the Holy Spirit ...Their poems are not private; they are images incarnated for themselves and for the community in which they live."
John Leax, American Poet

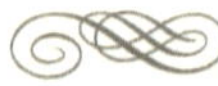

I'M OFTEN SURPRISED when I encounter the giftedness in others—not that they are resourceful, artistic, and inventive, but at the *ways* they express these traits from their Creator. What a blessing it is to look for imagination in the lives of people around me!

Friends, being a "real" artist isn't an exclusive private club made up of a few extraordinary people. I see your handiwork everywhere. Reset your mind to recognize art and creativity all around you, some of it made by your own hands or expressed by your own words—maybe when your kind encouragement hit a healing note in a wounded heart today.

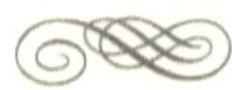

"The view of life I communicate in my pictures excludes the sordid and the ugly. I paint life as I would like it to be."
Norman Rockwell, American Painter, 1894-1978

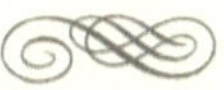

ONE OF MY FAVORITE passages about creativity in Scripture is recorded in Exodus 35, when Moses gathers the Israelites whose spirits prompted them to make offerings to create a "tent of meeting" for worshiping Him. *Their creativity was also to be an offering.* Notice the varied skills and vocations here in verses 10-19:

"Let all the skilled craftsmen among you come and make everything that the Lord has commanded: the tabernacle—its tent and covering, its clasps and planks, its crossbars, its posts and bases; the ark with its poles, the mercy seat, and the veil for the screen; the table with its poles, all its utensils, and the bread of the Presence; the lampstand for light with its utensils and lamps as well as the oil for the light; the altar of incense with its poles; the anointing oil and the fragrant incense; the entryway screen for the entrance to the tabernacle; the altar of burnt offering with its bronze grate, its poles, and all its utensils; the basin with its stand; the hangings of the courtyard, its posts and bases, and the screen for the gate of the courtyard; the tent pegs for the tabernacle and the tent pegs for the courtyard, along with their ropes; and the specially woven garments for ministering in the sanctuary—the holy garments for Aaron the priest and the garments for his sons to serve as priests."

When I read this passage, I smile. So many faces come to my mind—woodworkers, needle crafters, tanners, textile finishers, weavers, shepherds, horticulturists, bakers, sculptors, painters, mineralogists, jewelers, and so on. I wonder if the craftsmanship needed for the project encompassed all the skills represented in the tribes of Israel, so every person could feel involved. Their contributions were an offering made for God's glory, not their own reputation in their craft.

By the time we get to verses 30-35, Moses informs Israel that certain men have been Spirit-filled with wisdom, discernment, and abilities to create, direct, and teach others how to contribute to this amazing project.

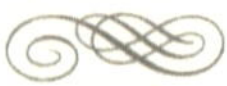

"Art is love."
William Holman Hunt, English Painter, 1827-1910

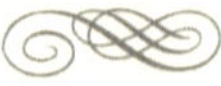

DO YOU LOVE TO COOK? That is how you can express and share your creativity. Do you like to decorate, organize, or pull together outfits to wear? You're innovative! Do you enjoy tinkering with machines, building things, gardening, sewing, or doing needlecrafts? You're inventive! Do you teach or care for children, the sick or elderly? Then you are drawing from deep resources of imagination to stay positive and give them hope and encouragement.

When I think back to the wonder and excitement of creative contributions that have blessed me, I recall the Vacation Bible School leaders and Sunday School teachers who relied on lesson plans written by crafts experts and donations from church members for craft time. As a child, my only art supplies at home were my pencils and notebook paper for school, crayons, and an imagination as big as the sky. My heart overflowed with joy as I toted my creations from classes at church back to give to my grandparents or my mom. Craft time, music time, and hearing about Jesus were my favorite things. When I was eight years old, and a pastor asked my class if we wanted to belong to Jesus, my heart almost burst with affirmation. I felt I'd always known Him, but I officially surrendered my life to Him that day in Vacation Bible School.

I don't remember the faces of the choir directors and music leaders that filled my childhood, but there is still no measure for how they blessed my life. My Gram-Gram (great grandmother) had a creaking rocking chair on the enclosed back porch of my Paw-Paw's house. With a Baptist Hymnal that had seen many years of handling before being replaced at church, I sat with open pages that were yellowed around the edges. I didn't know how to read music, but I'd memorized the main melodies of many songs I'd learned in the pews. One of my favorites was "Trust and Obey" (also known as "When We Walk With the Lord" by John H. Sammis and Daniel B. Towner, 1887). Maybe Jesus knew I'd need to internalize the theology and doctrine in that hymn. All I know is, to this day I can feel the rocker supporting me and creaking in accompaniment while I belted out the words to the song.

I could go on and on about all the people behind the scenes who nurture our inner desire to be creative or appreciate beauty, but this list makes my point. We are here to glorify our Creator, and part of that mandate is to reflect His attribute of creativity in ways unique to each of us.

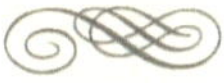

Nothing stays the same. Times will change, people in your life will come and go, and if you are abiding in Christ, He will redeem your bad experiences while you grow in spiritual maturity. This means you will move on to new interests, so you may pursue other creative avenues. It's all part of the plan for your contribution to the body of Christ.

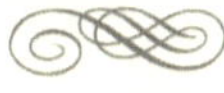

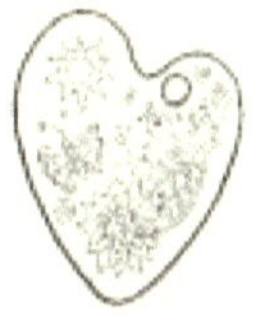

YOU HAVE A PURPOSE for existing and gifts to share for the time you are given to walk this earth. Few people ever find fame and fortune in their craft, but then, the glory isn't meant for us. Until around the time of the Renaissance, artists and artisans didn't sign their work for recognition, the way painters do today.

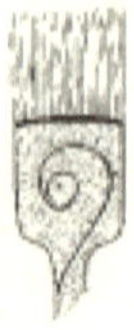

WHAT SKILLS, TALENTS, and hobbies are you sharing that bear the stamp of your Creator? Are you using them in ways that support the mind of your Maker for the good of those who love Him? Explain your answer.

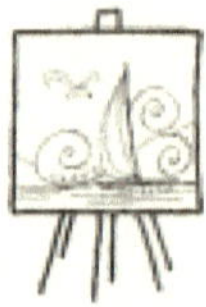

OUR GOAL AS CHRISTIANS is to do everything as if for the Lord (Colossians 3:23), and though we follow a calling, we may never gain public recognition for our creative pursuits. We find contentment, blessing, fulfillment, and pleasure in embracing the unique contributions He created us to make as part of the body of Christ.

Spirits in Conflict

"For we are His workmanship [poetry], created in Christ Jesus for good works, which God prepared beforehand so that we would walk in them."
Ephesians 2:10

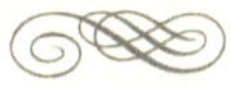

BASED ON EPHESIANS 2:10, and knowing we are endowed with unique gifts, *who decided what your dream is*? Why do you think so?

Christians should have an abiding relationship with Jesus so we will walk in step. (See John 8:31; John 15:4; 2 John 1:9; Galatians 2:20; Colossians 3:1-3). We need not strike out in relentless pursuit of our goals, and sometimes we need to surrender them and trust the timing to Jesus. Our personal strengths, interests, and hobbies are meaningful in being hard-wired within us.

Every day, we enjoy creativity provided by unbelievers. Our clothing, food, buildings, vehicles, etc. are brainstormed, designed, and crafted by people who don't follow Christ. In His wisdom, He used the skills of others to bless us, no matter their beliefs or lack of them—because the imprint of creativity is on each of us.

Sometimes, we get confused about whether we can enjoy the blessings provided by other people outside our Christian faith. I tried to untangle the ins and outs of this when I was a young mother who hoped to raise our children in a faithful home. We all must follow our own convictions when we seek the Lord's wisdom, and if this is an area you struggle with, I have no easy answer for you. I don't mind sharing some of my experience and conclusions, but as the Author Note in front of this book states, I'm in a state of growing maturity as a Christian, as we all are.

Let's look at the subject of music. The Bible's attention to this subject is impressive and includes varied styles and topics, such as worship, courtship and marriage, teaching, mourning, celebrations, warfare, pilgrimage, therapy, and pure pleasure. God created music for us, and He is glorified when we delight in His gifts. Musicians reflect the character of God when they arrange tones and rhythms for harmony. Songwriters and poets reflect His glory by composing meaningful lyrics that inspire our spirits to react to truth. Through Christ, mankind can appreciate and perceive the joys and complexities of music.

I've never believed music or songs must be Christian in theme or written as a hymn to be worshipful, for the source of worship is from within our hearts. In fact, some hymns and Christian songs are written by people with questionable beliefs and who fell away from the faith. Many of the popular new worship songs are focused on a Jesus we invented for ourselves, to meet our emotional neediness and our personal acceptance of what He will judge as sin or affronts to His majesty. I've heard interviews by band members in the Contemporary Christian music industry who reveal a surprising look behind the scenes, where many entertainers don't attend and outright reject church, and where there is no accountability or belief statement to adhere to. I'll be gracious when I say that several sources for worship music in churches today are in shaky territory at best when it comes to Biblical doctrine and themes.

Have you ever automatically been singing a well-loved old hymn and suddenly realized your heart and mind are not even engaged in worship? I have, and I try to re-focus on the precious words. Do you pay attention to the message in a song as you sing it to Jesus? I've sometimes stopped singing lyrics in the middle of a worship song on the radio or in a service because I realized they are unbiblical, or because the same lukewarm sentence is being repeated over and over.

With Christian music, I try to consider the fountain from which it springs—biblically, we are to hold fellow believers to accountability for doctrine and be watchful for false teachers. But it's impossible to know the salvation status and motivation for every source and every song we hear! So, my personal measure of any song is whether the lyrics reflect a biblical worldview.

With secular music, I expect musicians from many backgrounds to create songs that speak to hearts about life lessons. Rather than condemning all secular music, my family filters with limits for clean lyrics about non-offensive topics. Since everyone is created in God's image, much of life is experienced as universal truths. Scripture says the rain falls on the good and the evil, and He works to call souls to Himself. I could list rock star singers and band members who have made dramatic life changes by becoming Christians with riveting testimonies, but I'll just mention two examples. The former lead singer for Foreigner made this transformation. He once sang to celebrate having alcohol and drug induced double vision; now he's written a song about his single vision, Jesus Christ, and produced an album to celebrate Him. Back in the 1980s, the former lead singer for Kansas became a Christian and started working on winning his wife to the Lord. He wrote the song "Hold On" during that time.

The Bible is full of cautionary tales that aren't much different from mainstream secular songs. I'm currently journaling (again) through the book of Psalms. The sections on vengeance and calling people what they are, straight up, would never be acceptable in today's churches, though these are songs and prayers written in the Bible.

When we use discernment, many forms of music can bless us. All facets of human experience can be expressed through music. As I wrote my first novel, Painter Place, which is set in 1985, I planned to thread art, music, and creativity throughout the story (which became a series).

I wrote the book for myself, so I used my family's own guidelines for acceptable music. The standard for music the Painter family listens to or play at dances on the island is that there be no glorification of common vices like profanity, drugs, alcohol, sexual, etc. Yes, this means they listen to rock-and-roll if it passes the screening. They enjoy clean love songs, for there is a strong romantic language between lovers in the Song of Songs in Scripture.

At Painter Place, acceptable music is not determined by the state of salvation among the band members. The focus is on clean lyrics that speak to universal truth. Some of my readers have other music standards, just as they prefer versions of the Bible. I deeply respect their position.

I love to listen to relaxing instrumental ambient music, instrumental background movie soundtracks, Spanish acoustic guitar, and atmospheric music created for video games, etc. It's always on when I'm writing or painting. The beat moves me along, so I don't "stall out" in a project. Some of my sisters and brothers in Christ think this kind of music is out of bounds because there are also "new age" artists who create it, but if they'd listen to the stations and playlists I'm hearing, they'd encounter many famous composers and well-known hymns, as well as enchanting original compositions inspired by Scripture, performed by Christians like Stanton Lanier. Skilled musicians create beautiful, wordless inspirations that soothe me as I work, and I don't want lyrics to interfere with my communion with Jesus in my heart and mind as He inspires me.

Now, let's tie the controversial subject of music tastes into the theme of this chapter, "Spirits in Conflict." The point is that Satan will sidetrack us into extremes and deceive us into creating our own bondage about many things to keep us from accomplishing something for Christ's glory. The forces against Christ will attempt to prevent us from enjoying His gifts and blessings of common grace.

A Christian is God's reflection to the world. His enemy is our enemy.

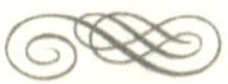

SHARING OUR CREATIVE efforts is a risk, a step of faith, like sharing the Gospel with someone. Creating and communicating something meaningful and beautiful requires courage. Christians must overcome the fear of criticism, rejection, and looking stupid.

Consider the examples we've covered so far in this book about the powerful ministry of creative thinking. Our spiritual enemy resists it. If you finish an inspired project, you've been blessed under Christ's favor, authority, and influence. That accomplishment and interaction with Him links you to His power to serve and change the world. In that way, the enemy's influence decreases every time you create something!

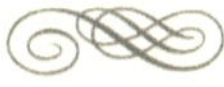

"If God gives you a few more years, remember, it is not yours. Your time must honor God, your activity must honor God, and everything you do must honor God."

A. W. Tozer, American pastor and author, 1897-1963

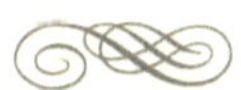

IF THINGS OCCUR TO stop your progress on a creative endeavor, don't assume you misunderstood. Wait on the Lord to clear the way and stay the course, unless you feel certain the project should be abandoned. Trust that you can either finish or benefit by what you learned up to that point. His timing will be perfect, and no spiritual attack can thwart His purpose.

My family and friends bear witness to the seasons of bizarre occurrences in our lives when I'm following a faith-themed project or teaching a class. I don't mean to sound spooky but after confirmation of a calling, things happen that we can only explain as spiritual attacks. My family expects this, so much so that when I discussed with my hubby my plans for writing an upcoming suspense series about spiritual warfare, he sighed and said we should put on our seat belts.

When we set our minds on things above, we prioritize our inspiration as an act of righteousness. We can expect the biblical concept of "increase" from it.

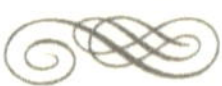

"His divine power has given us everything required for life and godliness through the knowledge of Him who called us by His own glory and goodness."
2 Peter 1:3

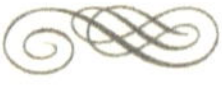

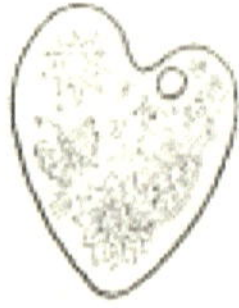

"YOU WILL KEEP THE MIND that is dependent on You in perfect peace, for it is trusting in You." Isaiah 26:3

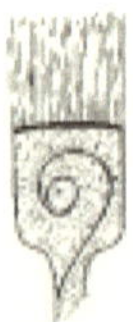

DO YOU PRAY FOR COURAGE and resolve to endure the conflict and resistance that Satan's spirit will bring against you during times of inspiration to complete a project? The greater the blessing to others in your work, the more the enemy will fight you. In December last year, I read the Book of Luke in the Gospels. I was struck by how often Jesus was confronting demonic activity and possession of people He encountered. This was sobering, but I also found comfort in the assurances of His power over His enemy.

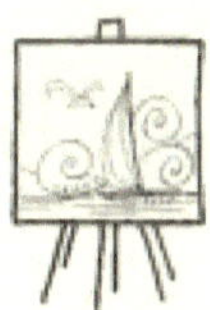

OUR CREATIVITY IS VALUABLE as we are shaped by Him and as we live wisely to make time for it. Creative initiative comes when we understand the power and dominion in creativity.

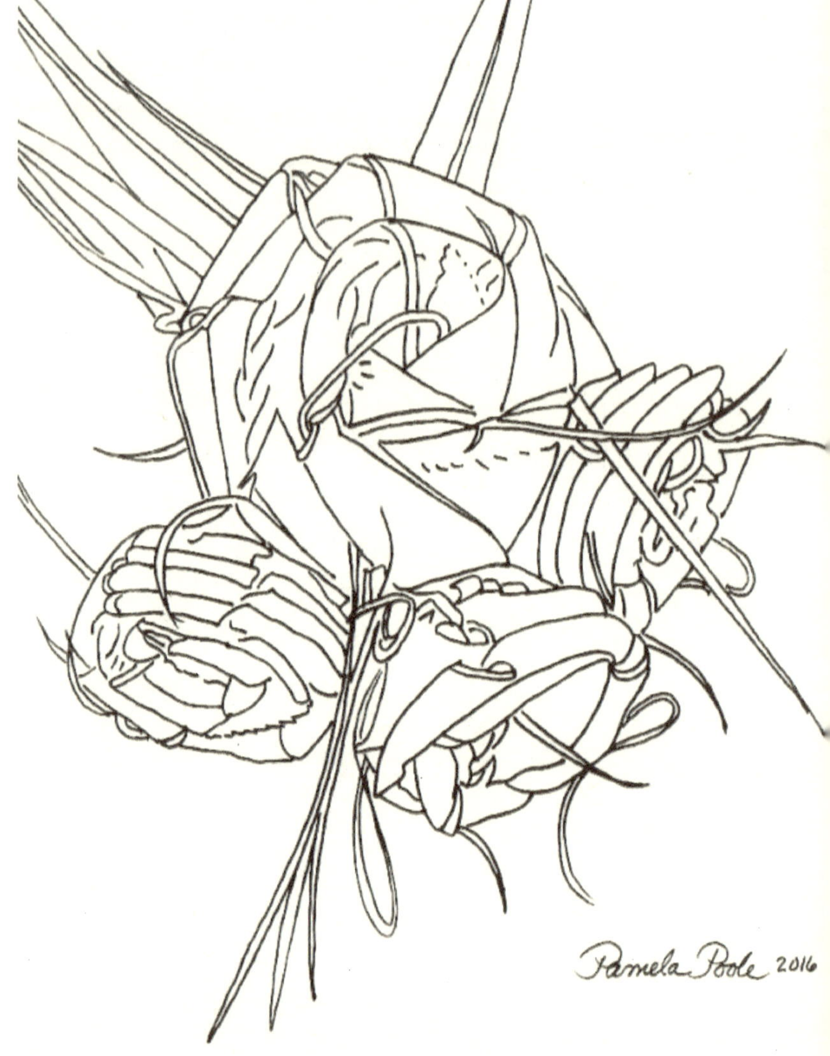

"Charleston's Palmetto Roses" Coloring Page

Contrasts: Beauty and Suffering

"Art, like morality, consists in drawing the line somewhere."
G.K. Chesterton, "The Illustrated London News," 1928

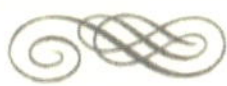

I ONCE READ THAT CHRISTIAN creative people should expect to suffer. The point of the statement was that those who look for beauty will necessarily have to contrast it with the surrounding ugliness. The contrast can't be reconciled because they spring from different sources, just as in scripture, where we're told that light has no fellowship with darkness. And to discern what light is, and what darkness is, we must make judgements based on Scripture. We must learn to see the line between the two.

But suffering isn't exclusive of those who seem to think and feel more deeply than others. All believers experience life's kaleidoscope of breathtaking awe and wonder, exhilarating joy, confusion, heartache, loss, loneliness, terror, and anxiety. Writing, painting, and singing about life means traveling dark roads. And if we walk with Christ, fulfilling the plans He has for us, we must expect spiritual battles, for that is how we become strong.

In the early chapters of the first book of the Bible, Genesis, we are given valuable information that establishes worldview foundations for believers. We learn why there is suffering in the world. We find out that man caused it, not God. Often, when I see mountains and canyons and recall how the worldwide flood of judgement in Noah's day caused the seas to scour the Earth, I praise my Savior that He turned the scars of sin and consequences into breathtaking beauty for us to marvel at. He's done the same thing in my heart!

The intuitive and observational gifts of many creative people impact their emotions more than an average person, but knowing what Scripture says leads all believers to healthy ways to cope and reach out with hope to others.

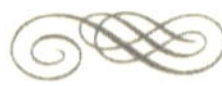

A problem-free life is a stagnant life.

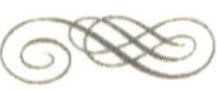

A LOOK INTO THE PASTS of many famous authors, artists, filmmakers, actors, and musicians reveals some ugly truths about suffering. Their biographies are about difficult relationships, addictions, devastating illness, loss, and suicide. People without Christ see only hopelessness for the future in the light/dark, beauty/vileness conflict. They communicate their worldviews about these challenges, and this infects the audience they have.

Contrast this with the glorious message of beauty, enduring love, forgiveness, and hope that fills books, film, and art created by Christians who have a mature spiritual outlook. If believers aren't discerning about the entertainment they consume and the art they enjoy, they will be misled into worldliness, false teaching that fits what they want to hear, and even despair when reality and consequences for waywardness must be faced.

I saw a sign for Columbia brand clothing and snapped a photo of it to remind myself of the universal truth in the words. It said, "Bad conditions make better stories." I laughed, not because I enjoy enduring bad conditions, but because I know for a fact that they make better stories. Readers expect me to put characters through situations with impossible odds, all for the entertainment of the audience!

Musically inclined believers weren't born to sing the blues. When they walk depressing paths, they find universal feelings to sing songs about. Listeners will be touched deeply in their souls, so don't leave them stuck in depression. Show them hope. The song "I Can Only Imagine" reminds me not only of my longing to see my little granddaughter and Paw-Paw, who are already home in heaven, but of the assurance that one day when I close my eyes here on earth, I'll open them to see Jesus for the first time. I have forever to be with Christ and my loved ones!

If you are a Christian who follows a creative calling, every aspect of your life—especially the suffering—can be a ministry, testimony, and outreach that does no harm to the Gospel of Jesus Christ. What message about Him are you projecting to the world?

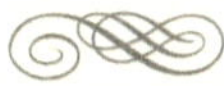

"All the masterpieces of art contain both light and shadow. A happy life is not one filled with only sunshine, but one which uses both light and shadow to create beauty."
Billy Graham, American Evangelist, 1918-2018

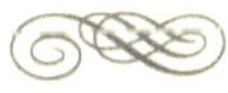

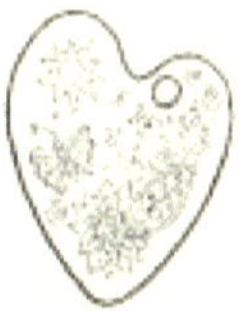

"FOR OUR MOMENTARY LIGHT affliction is producing for us an absolutely incomparable eternal weight of glory." 2 Corinthians 4:17

"Finally brothers, whatever is true, whatever is honorable, whatever is just, whatever is pure, whatever is lovely, whatever is commendable—if there is any moral excellence and if there is any praise—dwell on these things." Philippians 4:8

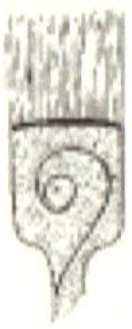

HOW HAS YOUR FAITH grown during the bad conditions that make your story better? Think of the last time you walked a dark road. Where did your light come from?

Knowing that the Christian walk requires discernment, do you choose your thoughts like you choose your friends?

A biblical understanding about how a perfect world became cursed will set us on solid ground for processing the contrasts in beauty and ugliness.

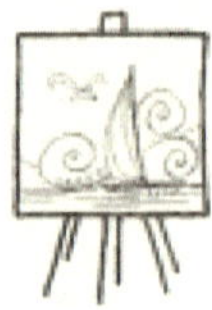

YEARS AGO, I WAS TEACHING a ladies' class at church and relating about our good and bad times in life. I told them how I didn't like painting or photographing outdoors on cloudy days because there were no shadows and colors were drab. Look for ways to appreciate the light and shadows in life.

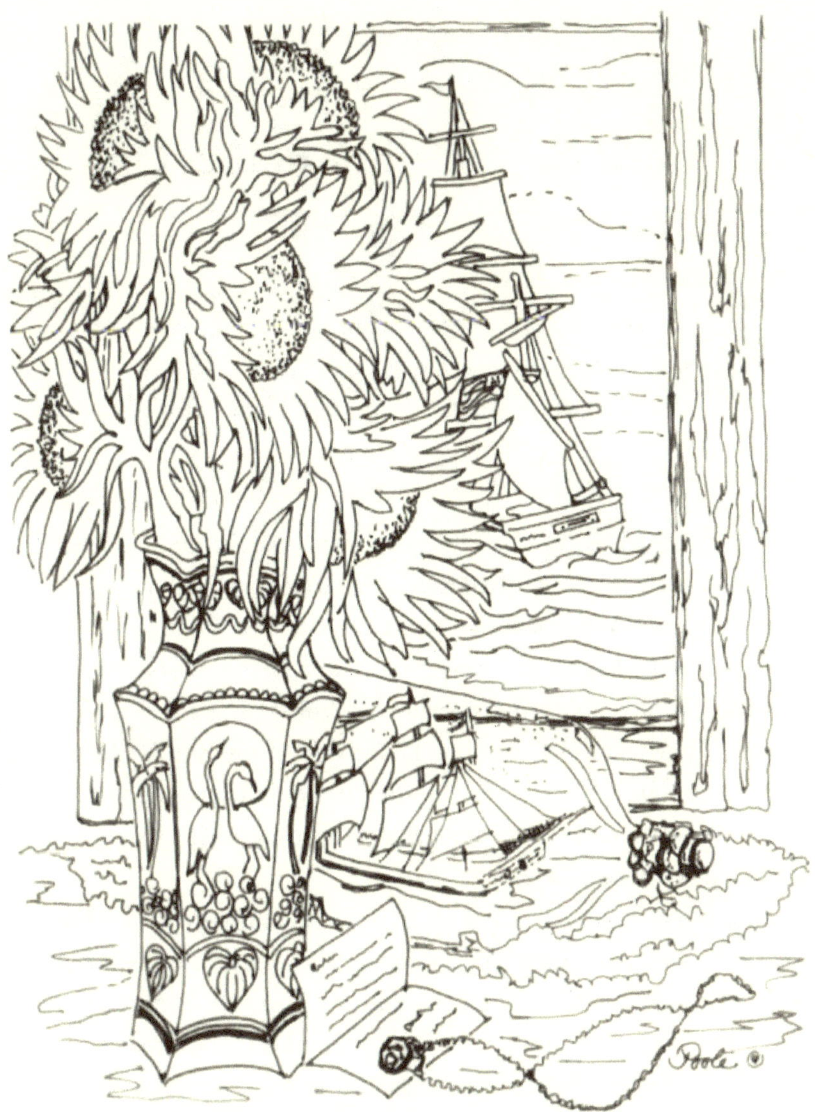

“Tall Ships and Sunflowers” Painter Place Cover Coloring Page

You'll Never Paint Another One

"No man ever steps into the same river twice—
for it is not the same river, and he is not the same man."
Heraclitus of Ephesus, Roman philosopher

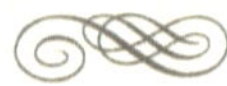

I ONCE OVERHEARD A long-time artist advise another one to always sell her work rather than hold on to a favorite for sentimental reasons. She said, "You can always paint another one."

Intuitively, I knew this well-meant advice was wrong. At the moment, I was busy with an organizational role in the art venue we were holding, but I couldn't get the advice out of my mind. On my way home, I thought through what bothered me about it, and a handful of years later, it came to mind as a great point to write into my first novel in the *Painter Place Saga*.

Caroline Painter is a young artist in a family in which only the artist of each generation inherits the major part of the small island in South Carolina that they've lived on for over three hundred years. In the following scene that illustrates my point about painting "another one," she's traveled to the English harbor town of Mevagissey in 1985 to help her uncle with filming an art video. The trip was supposed to help her get past a painful life change, but as an artist, it opened her emotions to try something bold and different.

"Most of you here know that an original painting is an interaction with an artist. Did you know that at any given time on any given day, the same subject matter by the same artist will be portrayed differently ac-

cording to moods and other influences? Sometimes, we paint a scene simply to share it and get people to look closer. Other times, we're working out something inside ourselves, the way people might talk things through with a friend to help them see more clearly. And at other times, the subject has special significance on a personal level."

Caroline paused, organizing her thoughts. "One of the terrific things about painting in acrylics is that they are dry enough to handle right after completion. I've painted three canvases in the past three days. Two of them were plein air views of the sea cliffs around Mevagissey, and they were experimental compositions. They fall into the category I mentioned about working things out as if we are talking them through, trying to understand them better. Imagine my surprise when the first one sold from the balcony of my room where I was painting it! The other one is titled Sea Cliffs and was done for filming here in the harbor yesterday."

She turned slightly to the canvas as Wyeth pulled the cover away. Guests showed their appreciation with applause and murmured comments. Facing their expectant expressions, Caroline hesitated, inhaling the air as if it contained courage. Then she remembered to smile.

"I created my next painting today in my room, after I was served a delightful Cornish breakfast at the inn and before dressing for this fabulous reception. It's an example of an artist choosing a subject for its special significance on a personal level, though it also involved working through a few things. This painting is inspired by the memories of a girl who always loved the sunflowers that grow around her home, and a boy who's fascinated at how the adventure of a tall ship can be contained in a bottle. Someone here tonight sent me sunflowers yesterday because they're my favorite flowers and he knew I'd be facing a challenging day. He knew how to show me he understands because he grew up watching me. I daresay he knows things about me I don't know yet myself."

You'll never be the same person when you "paint another one." In fact, if you painted the original with a passion that you worked out, nothing of it remains inside of you. You may trace over the same outlines of the original and transfer them to another surface, but frankly, if you do, you're missing the point of painting at all.

I'm not among those who believe creativity is about "self" expression. We should follow the Holy Spirit as He teaches us a gentle lesson about the subject. Along the way, we improve our skills.

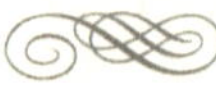

"Paintings have a life of their own that derives from the painter's soul."
Vincent van Gogh, Dutch Impressionist Painter, 1853-1890

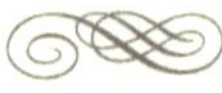

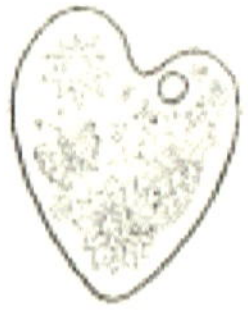

THE PERSON YOU ARE at this moment will be gone as quickly.

Each experience leaves us better or baser; neutrality isn't possible.

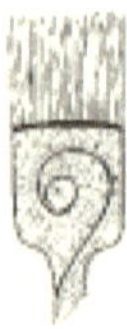

HAVE YOU NOTICED A change in your emotions or perspective after you've spent time in a creative activity? Vanna White, an American actress and celebrity from a popular game show, says crocheting helps her relax and saves her a lot of money in therapy. Christians can internalize the spiritual lessons in a creative activity while they build their skills.

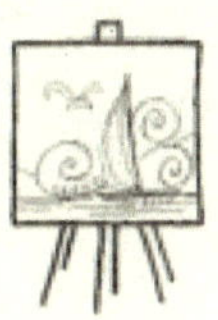

IF YOU DO NOT WANT to part with a painting or other craft you've made, there's a personal reason. Don't put a price on something that's priceless.

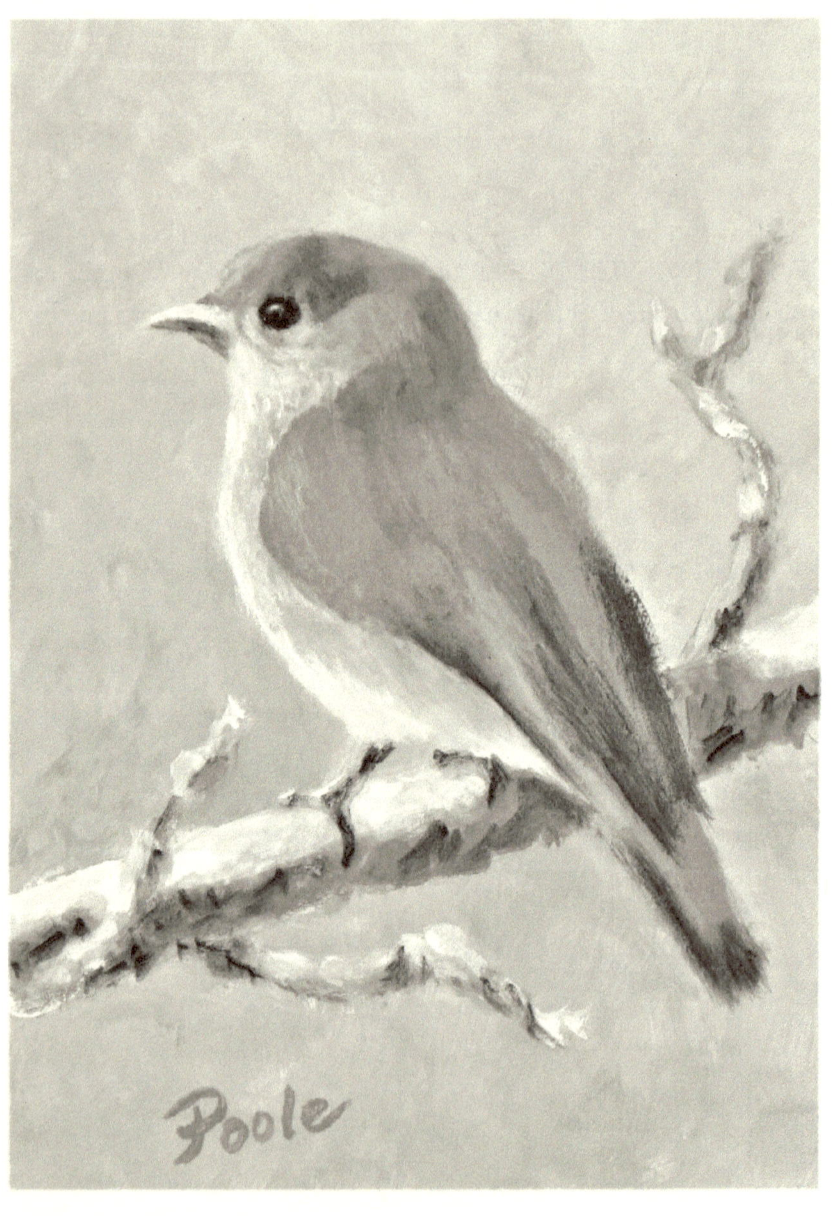
Poole

Erasing Mistakes

"As far as the east is from the west,
so far has He removed
our transgressions from us."
Psalm 103:12

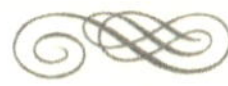

WHEN I DRAW OR PLAN out a sketch, an eraser stays in my hand. I use it often. Long ago, I got over the dream of being able to sketch confident strokes in ink that would be exactly right on the first try. The only artists who can do that put in far more time than I can to excel at this feat, and when they do, they are putting in far less time at something in which I excel.

I was both elated and horrified when art historians began using technology to see the underpaintings of famous art pieces. It was inevitable that failed attempts were covered over by the masters and enlightening that they rose above the shortcomings of their first attempts. A limited few of the renowned paintings by the master artists in history would become great works of art. Most were another step to the great paintings they dreamed of doing. Only the works of the undisputed genius of history, Leonardo da Vinci, are *all* considered masterpieces.

This is fine when the paintings being examined are by reputable artists whose art is worth millions. But my mind went to the bins where I store my paintings. Which ones hid a ghostly underpainting of the first clumsy effort, and could it be seen with an X-ray?

Like many artists, I go through my paintings now and then to throw out pieces that aren't my best work. Most of the paintings we hoped would be masterpieces were in fact only practice, and as we gain skills, we see this truth. Buyers may have appreciated those pieces at that point in our journey and have our paintings in their collections, but we don't want to leave inferior art behind in bins at home as our legacy. Part of becoming a good artist is learning to judge our work for what it is.

We may look back with embarrassment at entries we once put in shows, when we were hoping viewers and a judge would reward the work of our hearts, minds, and hands. Now we appraise the finished art from a more experienced perspective and realize our work can be inspired, yet not perfect. We do our best with the skill level we have—much like the way Jesus takes us as we are when we come to Him for salvation, then He stays patiently with us, helping us mature in our faith.

Our skills as artists and craftspeople improve with practice. If we are to move forward, we accept this as part of becoming more mature in our art and business.

Life is like this, isn't it? The more mature I become in my walk with Christ, the more regrets I have about the brokenness in my past. So often, my eyes have opened about something, and I've asked Christ why He let me speak, act on, or walk into something I'd later find was a mistake. If only I could erase or paint over some of it!

Scripture is full of the accounts of broken people who messed up. When I read about them, it's tempting to be aghast and say out loud, "God just did a miracle in his life! How could he turn around, take a step, and fall flat on his face?" Not only is there no eraser to clean up mistakes and no do-over to get things right, but those mistakes are recorded in the best-selling book in human history.

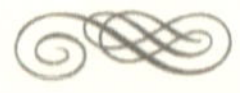

As much as I wish I could erase things about my life so the picture everyone sees is my best, that would be dishonest. The face I'm presenting right now is where I'm at in my spiritual walk with Jesus, and He is constantly working with me. The lessons along the way are all in the portrait. The most arresting part of the picture of me today had to be learned by walking through mountains, valleys, storms, and fire.

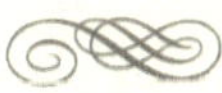

I HAVE CAUSED PAIN and hardship; I have suffered pain and hardship from others. I have been a blessing, and many others have blessed me. These experiences were points of growth in my life, layered like paint to create profound nuances of character in the portrait of who I am now. Some people will like what they see. Others will not. I am content with that.

Disciples of Christ need not concern themselves that He sees them like the portrait of Dorian Gray. On the day they trusted His word about their salvation, He washed their souls clean. If you struggle with assurance about who you are in His eyes, I urge you to talk to your pastor or do a Bible Study on the subject to get a proper perspective about your questions.

Regret about our past is a powerful tool used by Satan's forces to make us feel hopeless about moving forward with a purpose, looking toward the future. He taunts us about things that will never be erased. He does not want us to realize that as believers who walk with Christ, mistakes can become a riveting testimony that inspires others and draws the lost to salvation in Jesus.

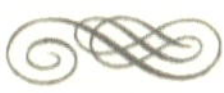

Be authentic. Your creativity places you in an arena to reach out, inspire, and touch an audience He will send to you!

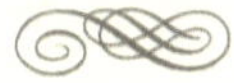

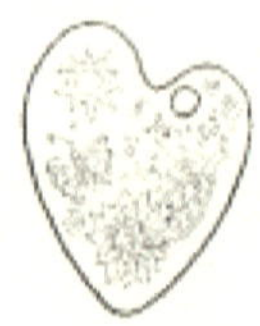

"BROTHERS, I DO NOT CONSIDER myself to have taken hold of it. But one thing I do: Forgetting what is behind and reaching forward to what is ahead, I pursue as my goal the prize promised by God's heavenlycall in Christ Jesus." Philippians 3:13, 14

"If we confess our sins, He is faithful and righteous to forgive us our sins and to cleanse us from all unrighteousness." 1 John 1:9

"As far as the east is from the west,
so far has He removed
our transgressions from us." Psalm 103:12

"And not only that, but we also rejoice in our afflictions, because we know that affliction produces endurance, endurance produces proven character, and proven character produces hope. This hope will not disappoint us, because God's love has been poured out in our hearts through the Holy Spirit who was given to us." Romans 5:3-5

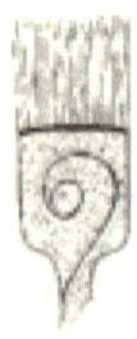

WERE YOU EVER HAUNTED with regrets? I hope that through Christ, you've been victorious and found peace. How has your faith cleared the way for you to accept His forgiveness and the paths He has planned for you? Authenticity makes you more approachable and your testimony more riveting. Can you think of a way Christ may use your life lessons in an opportunity to share?

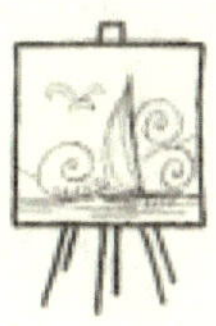

FINISHED PROJECTS ARE another step toward becoming better at your calling. They reflect who and where you are in your walk with Christ. They aren't masterpieces, but they still have power and influence for good.

Reaching Higher, Becoming Smaller

"The higher a man stands, the more the word vulgar becomes unintelligible to him."
John Ruskin, Art Historian

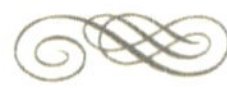

I ENJOY A BROAD RANGE of subject matter in art, including architecture. My favorite views of buildings are of porches to relax on and cottages by the sea, but churches also resonate with me. Pastoral settings with quaint churches evoke a sense of bygone eras when time passed slowly, and people were more reverent. These settings have an instinctive calming effect on people. Portrayals of lofty spires make me marvel at the creativity and ingenuity of humankind.

My family once had the honor of helping build a new sanctuary with the church we attended. We went to the site on the day when the steeple was being raised, and like other members of the congregation, we wrote scripture verses on the inside of the structure. Then, we watched as a crane lifted the steeple skyward and skillfully set it in place on the roof. I can't describe the feeling of participating in writing those carefully considered verses and knowing they rested over future congregations who would worship in the new sanctuary.

When I look skyward at church steeples, they remind me of a Bible verse in John 3:30. The steeples reach up as if touching heaven, pointing to the Lord as the highest person in existence. The spires tower over the body of believers inside the church, a reminder that they are citizens of heaven already and will go home someday. As a toddler, my Paw-Paw taught me to play a game with my hands. He helped me clasp my fingers together toward my palms and create "doors" with my thumbs joined side by side. We'd say, "Here's the church..." then he'd have me raise my forefingers to touch in a point and continue, "...here is the steeple..." and we'd turn my hands up to "...come inside and see all the people!" I'd wiggle the "people" in the various sizes of my fingers.

Church steeples remind us to look up at the only thing that ultimately matters, far and away above all our fleeting concerns on earth. The spire decreases into a point that ends in the heavens, and yet we are the ones who feel small.

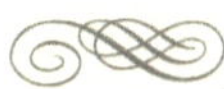

"You will keep the mind that is dependent on You in perfect peace, for it is trusting in You." Isaiah 26:3

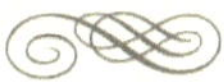

SOMETHING I LOVE ABOUT looking into the sky is that there is so much *still space*. Even when a storm threatens, a vast, open area surrounds the lightning and creates the stage for the electricity.

Two artists whose work I admire are both Americans, Howard Pyle (1853-1911) and his student, N.C. Wyeth (1882-1945). These men dominate storytelling painting because of the knockout punch they used so effectively: the element I call **still space.** Also referred to as "white" or "negative" space by art teachers, still space is the first thing I teach students. Until they grasp that vital art element, they either draw an image in constricted small spots on their sketch paper or else fill the page with what I call "too much muchness."

While learning to use space as an art element also includes learning more advanced concepts, such as depth and perspective, still space is understood when we recognize the ***restful*** area between, around, above, below, or within objects. It's the background to enhance and spotlight the core subject of a painting. If it's full of distractions, an artist loses the impact of leading viewers to the focal point. In the example I started with, a stormy sky, the lightning is so dramatic because the surrounding area is so much the same.

How does this interesting art lesson illustrate the point I started with—that church steeples draw our eyes heavenward? *Because busyness is a creativity killer, and our souls are starving for still space.* When our eyes are on the world, it's impossible to see beyond ourselves.

We desperately need to look up and remember who blessed us with the gift of another day. We should be seeking peace in our souls to listen to Jesus. The closer we get to Him, the less there is of us and the more we are like the only perfection that exists.

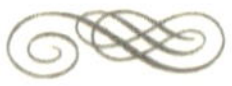

"He must increase, but I must decrease."
John 3:30

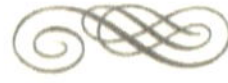

HAVE YOU HEARD THE account of how Leonardo da Vinci diminished the expertise he could have displayed in his painting "The Last Supper" to keep the focus on Jesus? The artist faced many challenges while painting the 15 feet by 29 feet painting on the dining hall wall in a convent in Milan, Italy in 1495-1498. Though there are many art and faith elements to note in this masterpiece by the undisputed genius in history, I wanted to illustrate the artist's willingness to step back from his own notoriety so the impact of the painting's message would remain uppermost in the minds of viewers.

Da Vinci invited one of his confidants to critique the painting as it dried. His friend was captivated with Da Vinci's depiction of the chalice which Christ would have touched to his lips that night with the disciples. He noted that the ornate cup, embellished with gold and glimmering with jewels, was worthy of the service it would have provided in the scene.

When his friend left, the artist painted over the cup with the humble one we see today. When his friend asked why he'd eliminated that splendid part of the painting, Leonardo da Vinci said, "Nothing must distract from the figure of Christ."

In what ways are we more focused on building a name for ourselves and showing our expertise instead of using our influence to point others to Jesus?

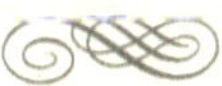

"Nothing must distract from the figure of Christ."
Leonardo da Vinci, 1498

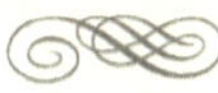

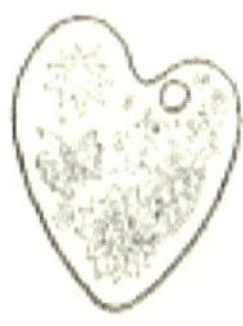

"BUT YOU ARE A CHOSEN race, a royal priesthood, a holy nation, a people for His possession, so that you may proclaim the praises of the One who called you out of darkness into His marvelous light." 1 Peter 2:9

"One thing have I asked of the Lord, that will I seek after: that I may dwell in the house of the Lord all the days of my life, to gaze upon the beauty of the Lord and to inquire in his temple." Psalm 27:4

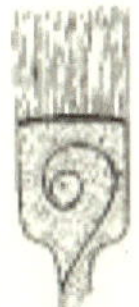

DID YOU KNOW THAT BEFORE the Renaissance Era, it wasn't common for an artist to sign his work? This changed with a new emphasis on individual skills and differentiated better artists from their peers. Today, it is a common practice because collectors look for a signature and artists are protected for copyrighted work.

Have you ever considered whether you seek recognition and acclaim for yourself in your creative pursuits? If you do, can you be content if fame and fortune never comes from it? There is nothing wrong with sharing our latest project on social media and with friends, putting it on our websites for sale, and promoting it on a market. We may be called to be salt and light in the world by sharing our work. The real key is to keep a proper perspective of our part in the project. It's not ultimately about us, nor is it about an audience.

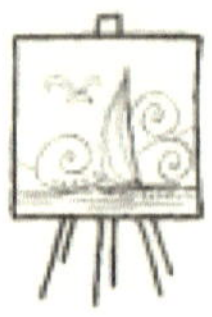

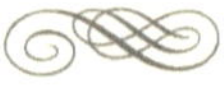

WHETHER YOUR EXPRESSION of creativity is "religious" in theme or if it's a crocheted cap for the preemie intensive care unit at your local hospital, it should be done for Christ.

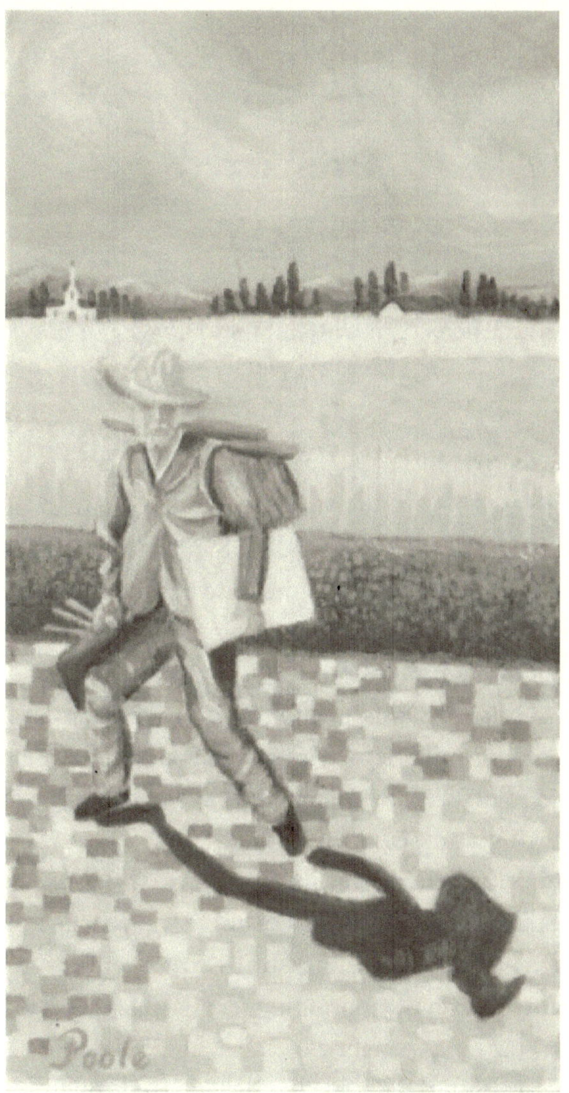

"Vincent the Painter in Arles"

Convicted

"So it is a sin for the person who knows to do what is good and doesn't do it."
James 4:17

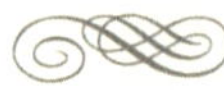

WHEN WE ACCEPTED CHRIST'S gift of salvation, we changed our mind about sin. His Spirit came to live in us and started remodeling. We have an entirely new way of seeing and understanding, as if we walked into another dimension.

Scripture describes this phenomenon as holiness and assures believers of their new inheritance in heaven, paid for by the sacrifice and cleansing blood of Jesus. Recognizing your righteousness in His eyes is the key to having a proper self-image.

Jesus takes us where we are when we surrender our souls to Him—we can never "clean up" to qualify as good enough. Since that starting place is different for each of us, every journey is unique. We must face our traditions, upbringing, environment, personalities, and other circumstances as we get closer to Him. He doesn't force us. We will come to see things we valued and clung to through His eyes, then we willingly let them go.

I've come to a difficult chapter for myself in this devotional. Using my life to illustrate my theme is risky, for readers will receive the message as being either authentic or arrogant.

I could use examples from others who shared things like this publicly, but it's time to speak from my own experiences. Until now, only close family members and perhaps a friend have ever heard these stories. But in Christ, nothing is wasted. Everything has a time and a purpose, and now readers will see that in writing this devotional, I'm not parroting all the things I've learned in church about living on a higher plane than the world. I know how hard it is to grapple with conviction, testimony, and reputation.

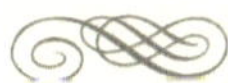

As a Christian who decides to follow a calling to go public with your creative endeavors, you will face a sense of isolation and a longing for like-minded friends.

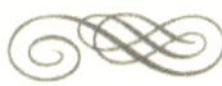

THROUGHOUT MY YEARS of participation and leadership in artist venues, I've experienced a range of reactions to my personal convictions as I walk with Christ. I follow Peter's advice in 1 Peter 3:15-16, studying and knowing how to explain my faith and why I don't walk the easier, broader paths most people are on—yes, even many Christians.

As an artist and author, after much prayer, I've chosen to share some of my creative work on the markets. In doing so, I braced myself for brutal criticism and resolved to walk publicly as an ambassador for Christ. My personal faith conviction about not drinking alcohol limits which opening receptions I attend; my conviction about nude art limits which exhibitions I can enter; the biblical worldview of my novels limits my audience for sales and reviews; and my testimony limits how I can socialize with other artists and authors.

When I was part of an art gallery, my convictions were tested when a new member began bringing in nude art. When my solo exhibit month came up, the gallery's only display space at the time was beside his work on the same wall. Until my contract was up, I had no power to change this, and while I was obligated as a member to distribute some postcards about the reception to a few bulletin boards, I didn't publicize or invite people to my exhibition. (For more on this subject, see "The Figure" in the next chapter in this devotional).

In the same gallery, I signed on with the understanding that I do not drink wine and would not serve it, yet, when my only reception duty came up, of course the artist who served had to step away and a visitor asked me for wine. Fortunately, it was poured and sitting on the refreshment table. When my contract was up a couple of months later, I was relieved. During my time in the gallery, I sold paintings and had a private commission, but I loaded my paintings into my car.

For the record, there is no correlation between alcohol and art sales. In fact, when we lived in Charleston, there was a genuine problem with crowds in galleries for wine and champagne receptions, so much so it made the news when galleries brainstormed solutions. Many attendees came only for the social aspect and to get free drinks and food—especially the college students. My hubby and I were among many who stopped attending Art Walk evenings to see the work of my friends because groups of people gathered to talk in the walkways and blocked foot traffic to see the art. After attending several receptions on the same street, party goers were saturated, sloppy, and loud. No one was thinking about or buying art.

I once attended a terrific pastel painting workshop in Charleston with a well-known artist I admire. Since my family had recently moved away from Charleston, I stayed in the area for the week. Some other artists kindly included me in an invitation to go to a rooftop bar after class, which I respectfully declined but offered heartfelt thanks for their thoughtfulness. When asked if I had other plans, I was honest in explaining that I'd get dinner somewhere alone, since bars were off limits because of my reputation and convictions. This led to another question, and I explained that I was an art teacher of Christian homeschooled students and taught women's groups at church.

The next morning, one lady in the group came over to me in the parking lot as I unloaded my easel and supplies to paint plein air along Shem Creek. In honest curiosity, she asked about my testimony. I told her I used to live in Charleston and if someone I knew, such as a former student or fellow church member, saw me out at a bar with a group of people that didn't include my husband, assumptions could ruin my influence as a Christian. Also, it would be disrespectful of my husband's role in my life, since men in a bar setting might think I was available. And finally, even if I only carried a glass of water, many drinks are clear. Drinking alcohol is against my Christian convictions. In short, it was not a setting I could socialize in because of my testimony in Christ.

She was gracious and I silently thanked Jesus for a chance to reach out. That evening was the best one I've had in an artist workshop, for the leader and his wife took us all out on a tour of the historic streets of Charleston and taught us how to use our cameras for dramatic night photos for future paintings.

The culture has grown even darker in the years since then, however, and I've stopped joining local artist and author groups because of a yawning gap in like-mindedness. There's no reason for Christian artists to put themselves in the position of conforming to whatever trending social vice may be required of them as members and participants. I carefully screen any exhibitions before showing my work there, and I interview the organizers of workshops for well-known artists before attending. Buyers don't purchase art because the painting won recognition in shows, and I need no art critic's affirmation for my work. After being in leadership positions to witness the biases of art show judges, I learned years ago not to place importance on awards. I watched one exhibition being judged by a woman whose beloved cat had died the day before. Predictably, every painting with a cat in it was a winner, no matter the artistic value of the other paintings. In fact, one member won two awards for her cat paintings, and the guild had to vote to make a new rule that members could only win one award per show.

In mostly female artist guilds and Christian author groups, even in a large national Christian Fiction association, I've found there is little consideration shown for the members who are offended by profanity and crudeness. Artist groups don't unite as believers, so I expect a secular situation when I interact with them. But Christian authors are different. They are held to a higher standard as believers. In my experience, many of them feel they must be edgy in romance and use the language of the lost—profanity—to communicate with today's readers. Yet, I've heard and seen no testimonies about anyone who was led to Jesus because someone used the language of the streets and gutters.

Back in 2019, I saw a post on a Facebook page for avid readers of Christian fiction. Someone told of her horrible experience with fiction full of cursing and a very detailed sex scene. She had chosen the audiobook because it was in the Christian category, and she expected a clean story with some faith elements. But she had to stop listening. In her post, she asked other readers if this is common.

The comment thread was long and growing longer by the minute. I scrolled through to see the reactions and will return to it later. Sadly, many readers vented that they are encountering the same disappointment and departure from expectations in Christian fiction. They also report that among the clean stories in this category, characters don't live like believers and there is barely a nod at faith.

This group of readers is a cross section of my audience. I feel bad for them. And I'm one of them! Being an author was not my dream. I'm an author because my son challenged me to write the books I want to read and can't find.

Remember back in an earlier chapter of this book, *Embracing Your Calling*, when we looked at how the Israelites were to employ their creative skills as an offering to the Lord? Shouldn't modern believers view their creative efforts that way? This is a conviction for me and was never more important than when I started communicating through novels.

I already had two novels published before I attended my first and only Christian women's writer retreat. After arriving at the beach location, I learned that we would all introduce ourselves and launch into our initial topic, about how Christian publishers were accommodating modern authors. They would do this by relaxing their rules to allow language that had been traditionally unacceptable. My heart sank as we moved on, going around the room to introduce ourselves and talk about how we became authors or what inspired us to write.

When it was my turn, I explained that I started writing the books I wanted to read but couldn't seem to find, free of foul language and having a meaningful story with characters who lived Christian worldviews. I related that I'd seen the conflict my son encountered in Christian writer groups online who argued to justify cursing and crude language to be relevant and realistic, and that I avoided those groups because Scripture clearly warns in many passages that believers watch their mouths and avoid thinking and talking like the world. Instinctively, I lifted my hands as if holding out a gift, and explained that my creative work represented an offering for my Savior, free from things that would not bring glory to Him.

Many of you know how it feels when an awkward silence falls on a group after something you've said, so I won't describe it. But I was calm and had peace from saying the right thing in the wrong place. The other ladies told their stories of how they came to be writers, and we took a break.

One leader took me aside to show me her blog, where I was exposed to many of the words I avoid. Providentially, an attendee came to my rescue, interrupting her by telling me how much she admired my testimony of becoming a writer and asking more about ministries my husband and I were involved in. And in another session, an attendee lifted her hands as I had when she said she considered her work to be an offering to the Lord, too. The topic about offensive language in our work didn't come up again that weekend.

It was an awkward couple of days, but I believe Christ was building a foundation in my creative life and outreach. I was in the familiar territory of not fitting in, but He affirmed my convictions and solidified my resolve.

After a year of disappointment, I cut ties with a state chapter of a Christian national organization for authors. The last meeting that I attended was when the guest speaker was an award-winning author with a Christian publisher. She writes fiction about biblical characters. But that day, she cursed as part of her presentation, and covered her mouth with a mocking, unapologetic expression—and looked straight at me. Perhaps my reputation had spread.

In that instant, I felt a passing grief for that author and for the damage she'd done to her testimony. I felt sad for what the writer support group might have been. And I felt a twinge of loneliness. But I also felt freedom, the urge to shake the dust from my feet and move along.

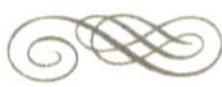

"No foul language is to come from your mouth, but only what is good for building up someone in need, so that it gives grace to those who hear."
Ephesians 4:29

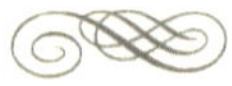

AS THE CHRISTIAN READERS' group on Facebook pointed out, foul language isn't the only thing they shouldn't find in fiction written for Christian audiences. If you're a reader and you're interested in a Christian worldview on romance, you might enjoy two blogs on the Southern Sky Publishing website. They are, "Is It Real? 7 Keys for Writing Romance for Christians" and "Realities About Romance In Christian Fiction And Why It Matters."

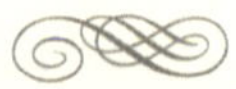

"I'd rather know what's what than be listed in Who's Who."
Pastor Adrian Rogers

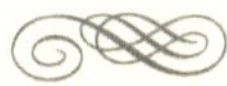

ART AND OTHER CREATIVE activities are not intended to be vehicles for bringing worldliness into our lives, and membership in guilds or groups is not a ticket to a mission field. If we gain skills that take our work to a higher level by participating in a group or a workshop, there may be an opportunity for outreach to those who ask why our convictions are different. If we are abiding in Christ and seeking direction, He may lead us there to accomplish a purpose. But He may also lead us out again to more like-minded relationships. The Bible warns about the company we keep. We are associated with the personality of our networks and are more likely to be corrupted than to change corruption. (See verses such as 1 Corinthians 15:33-34; Ephesians 4:17-18; Psalm 1:1-2; Proverbs 1:10; Proverbs 4:14-15; Exodus 23:2.)

Do you find it difficult to find like-minded fellowship in groups? Then perhaps your only companion is supposed to be Jesus at this season of your life. Never be ashamed of Jesus or Scripture and don't fold up when you should stand up to leave a situation. Know what you believe and be ready to share your testimony.

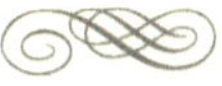

"Praise the God and Father of our Lord Jesus Christ, who has blessed us in Christ with every spiritual blessing in the heavens."
Ephesians 1:3

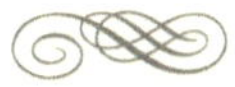

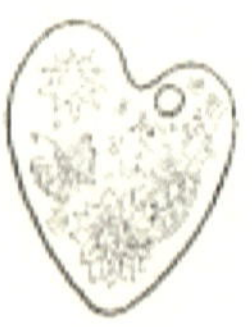

"AND WHATEVER YOU DO, in word or in deed, do everything in the name of the Lord Jesus, giving thanks to God the Father through Him." Colossians 3:17

"Therefore, I say this and testify in the Lord: You should no longer walk as the Gentiles walk, in the futility of their thoughts." Ephesians 4:17

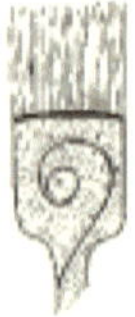

HAVE YOU CHANGED THE way you live by changing the way you think? We can't do it on our own. But we can pray for the grace and guidance needed so that our associations, conduct, and creativity are led and inspired by the Holy Spirit.

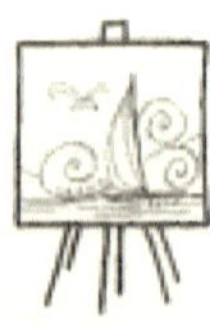

COMMITMENT TO A CALLING means you won't hesitate to testify about Jesus and apply scripture to your accomplishments. Whether your work is "religious" or universal in theme, your life is a public reflection of Christ.

The Figure

"The Lord God made clothing out of skins for Adam and his wife, and He clothed them."
Genesis 3:21

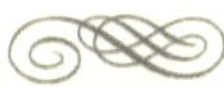

IN A WEEKLY OPEN STUDIO that I took part in a few years ago, some female artists were sharing among themselves about being in a figure drawing group. They rolled their eyes at the fact that male members of the society only attended if there was a nude model.

I don't bring up figure drawing or painting in art circles unless I must. It's exhausting to explain my convictions. Even attendees who consider themselves Christians might say that nude drawings and paintings don't bother them and glorify the innocence mankind once had by portraying the beauty of the bodies the Lord created. They will point out masterpieces in art history as if those painters were the ultimate authority on morality, rather than the authority of Scripture in Genesis 3:21, when God thought it was important to clothe Adam and his wife.

Do you believe there's a difference between paintings, drawings, and sculpture of the unclothed human figure compared to what we consider being pornography? Do you think the men in the figure drawing group I mentioned saw a difference? Why or why not?

For this chapter, I researched the latest statistics about the cultural impact of viewing nude and almost nude images, and I'll call it what it is: pornography. The numbers about youth and teens were frightening, but since this devotional is for professing Christian adults, that will be my focus group.

Covenant Eyes, a filter for families for online accountability, states that 56 percent of divorce cases involved a partner's obsessive interest in porn sites. In addition, 64 percent of Christian men and 15 percent of Christian women report watching porn at least once a month. This is a departure from the teachings Christians adhere to in their worship. (Source: Fox News, January 2019).

As believers, we must ask ourselves if our creativity leaves our audience better or baser. Do our creations minister to, or build up, the body of Christ, for His glory?

To illustrate how a Christian might handle this topic, I'm including an excerpt from my third novel, Jaguar. The artist is Caroline Painter, the main character, code named the Princess in the rescue mission. It summarizes her biblical worldview about the human figure in art.

The Puma grinned. "I assumed artists liked to do portraits and considered nudes to be an intellectual pursuit that the general population was too crude to appreciate."

The Jaguar snorted. With a one-sided smile, the Princess replied, "I include people in some of my scenes, but I'm not a portrait artist. People are demanding and complicated. I try to depict the quiet solitude of places to escape from a noisy, demanding world."

She stared into the flames as they began to burn low. "I never do nudes and won't show in an exhibition that includes them. They're an oddity that distracts from the other paintings hanging nearby. Even a child knows by instinct that it's not appropriate. People don't sit around like that—it's a contrived setting, and there are laws against public nudity. It offends people. Anyway, God's very clear in scripture about His view of that issue. Other artists have argued with me that if there's a God and He created people with nothing on, then we should relish the beauty of the human form. But they twisted the Genesis account and didn't consult the rest of the Bible for context."

She paused when the Jaguar stopped the soft strumming on the guitar to listen. Seeing that they all stared and waited, she continued. "Adam and Eve's choice to sin changed everything. They lost their privilege of walking with God in Eden, so perhaps they missed the covering of light that shines over those who spend time with Him. Whatever was lost about their appearance, it was dramatically different if it made them so afraid. It was also unacceptable to God, who killed the first animal to cover them with its skin. It was a picture of the Lamb to be slain to cover their sin, when Christ came to the world for that purpose and died. If God Himself thought the only two people in the world needed to be clothed, then you can bet it's important. The rest of scripture always associates nudity with shame, except within marriage. When the sinless environment of heaven is mentioned, as in Revelation—I think it's in 1:13 and 19:14—we're all wearing white robes to signify innocence."

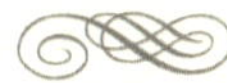

"The armies that were in heaven followed Him on white horses, wearing pure white linen." Revelation 19:14

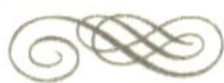

SO, IF BELIEVERS HAVE this mindset, how can they avoid nudity in art? It's difficult. When I was teaching my son and other students for a high school credit in art history, I handpicked the paintings of popular master artists. I also attached sticky notes to pages in books. Some kids laughed, knowing why I covered those parts of the pictures, which is a proof that even children know artists have gone too far and disrespected the human body.

When I visit art museums, I look away from paintings that glorify nudity. Philippians 4:8 makes it clear what my mind should dwell on. What edification and benefit would there be for my life, relationships, and faith if my eyes lingered, and I walked through the doors of imagination that the artist opened for me?

It's difficult to look over novels on the book markets without being assaulted with images of bare-chested men and immodestly dressed women on the brink of needing a room. These covers entice and excite, and while not approved for "clean" and Christian markets, I often find the same worldly dating situations in steamy descriptions within the contents of the Christian books. Should Christian writers be enticing believers to let their minds wander to what happens next between these unmarried couples? How does this bring glory to God?

In my fourth novel, Landmark, I wrote a scene to help readers see a creative solution that worked out for my main character, an artist named Wyeth Painter. Here is how he handled the situation when he was faced with a required university art class assignment to create a painting from a unclothed model.

"In college, an art professor of mine was determined to give me a failing grade for figure painting if I didn't come to class and paint a nude. He made it his mission to free me from my oppressive religious upbringing. So, I asked if I could get credit if I proved I understood the human frame by hiring and painting a dancer to model for me, wearing a leotard and a clinging skirt. Phillip went with me to the library to study up on the female muscular system beforehand, which was difficult to do without running across much more information than we'd seen in Biology class. Then he and a female art student friend of ours sat with me to sketch the model while I painted. My professor relented and gave me credit for 'an outstanding depiction of athletic grace.'"

How did you come to your current view about figures in your art, books, and entertainment? What source of authority guided your decision? Explain your answer as if you are speaking to fellow believers, using Genesis 3:21. Compare your position on this subject to what is accepted as popular by society's standards. Is there a worldview about nudity that contributed most to pornography addiction and the divorce statistics that polls tell us?

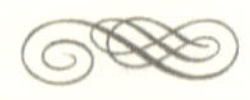

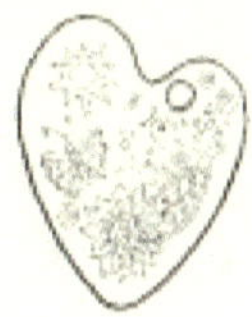

"DO NOT LOVE THE WORLD OR the things that belong to the world. If anyone loves the world, love for the Father is not in him. For everything that belongs to the world—the lust of the flesh, the lust of the eyes, and the pride in one's lifestyle—is not from the Father but is from the world. And the world with its lust is passing away, but the one who does God's will remains forever." 1 John 2:15-17

"The Lord God made clothing out of skins for Adam and his wife, and He clothed them." Genesis 3:21

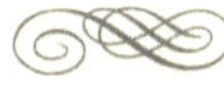

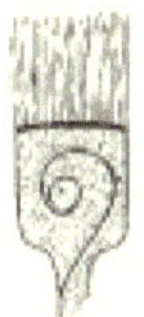

HOW DOES YOUR CREATIVITY contribute beauty that glorifies righteousness and points to the pure white linen in our real home, heaven? Explain your answer.

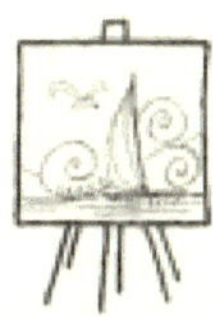

DECIDE WHO YOUR AUTHORITY is about morality in art and entertainment, specifically about depictions of the figure.

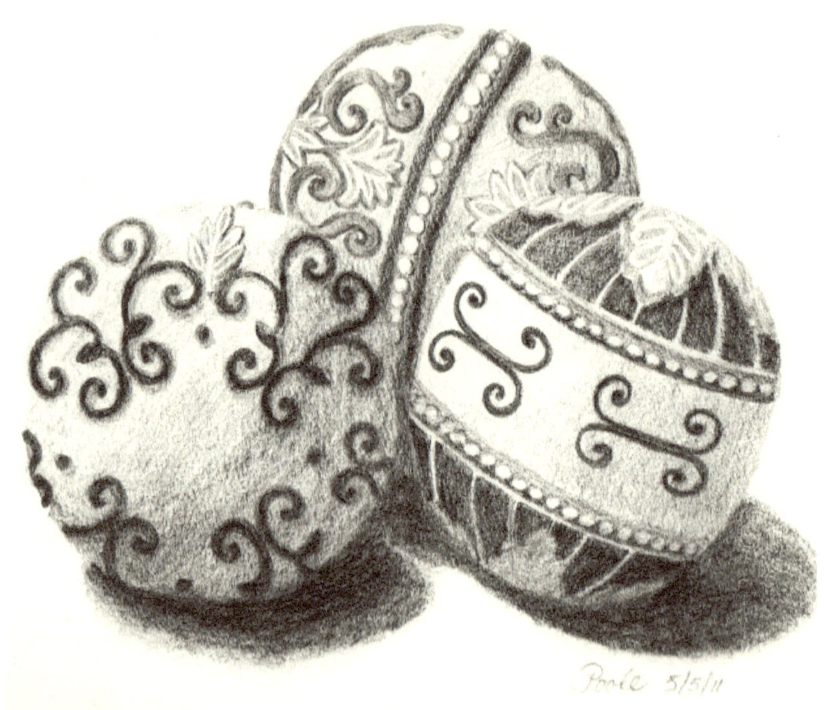

"Renaissance Globes"

Ethics and Originality

"There was no one near to confuse me,
so I was forced to become original."
Franz Joseph Hayden, Father of the Symphony

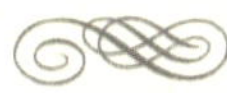

BEING INSPIRED AND communicating about the Lord doesn't mean He leads us to depict religious themes in our creativity. But our redemption includes our abilities and is vital in our testimony. We must be mindful of our ethics and business practices.

One contentious issue I've often had to deal with in the realm of art and photography is a disregard for the rules of originality and exhibition. But if your creativity runs to crafts, woodworking, and other skills for exhibits in venues such as the State Fair, don't skip out on this section. When an artist enters a competition or group, he or she bears the responsibility of abiding by the rules. There is no excuse, and it isn't necessary to suffer the frustration and embarrassment of being disqualified.

In terms of being a member of an arts or crafts group, study their rules for participation. Ask questions. This includes online venues, so don't skip over the membership pages and fine print.

Now for the most universal rule, and this mostly concerns images (paintings, photographs, etc.). Be sure you know the standards expected for true originality as an artist. This is not open to interpretation by the artists themselves. It is the leveling factor of expectations for a fair playing field for everyone.

There are some easy ways to remember why the rules for originality make sense, without hashing through the ins and outs of copyrights (though that is a big deal that can end in a lawsuit). Eventually, an aspiring artist will come to understand how important *composition* is to a painting. Composition will trump artistic technique any day with a good art show judge. The skill of designing great compositions can take years to master and is a part of the vision attributed to an artist.

Outside input about paintings, such as an instructor's advice and critiques from other professionals, also lends an unfair advantage to an artist when they enter such a painting into a competition. Copying can be helpful in the learning process, but has no place when artists are expected to be standing on their own merits.

This is where we can come to the bottom line in understanding originality. Photos may be a reference, such as to understand the anatomy of a flower when an artist is painting one and runs into trouble. But using a photo that is not an artist's own as the subject for a painting, including copyright-free stock photos, means that the artist has used someone else's composition, and therefore taken advantage of a shortcut to what may well be the successful part of the painting. This isn't an acceptable way to present oneself as a professional artist with integrity.

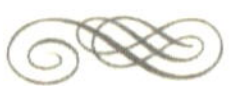

The hardest thing and the right thing are often the same thing.

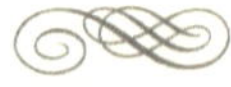

ONE OF THE MOST MEMORABLE stories I can use to illustrate how important it is to understand originality and following exhibition rules is from my personal experience. When I took on the leadership role as president of an artist guild, I surrounded myself with an exceptional team of officers. Old-timers were coming back and happy about the fresh energy. Then one day, my latest issue of an art magazine came in the mail with winners of a national competition. Soon afterwards, the magazine had to take away one winner's award and declare that the artist had broken the entry rules and copied a photograph. Around the same time, I got a call from my guild officers to let me know that one of our members had won an award in a huge local exhibition and copied the *same photo* as the artist that was disqualified in the national art magazine! Two other members had questionable award-winning paintings in the same show.

I dreaded going to the venue and meeting with the director, a friend from my Sunday School Class. It was embarrassing to explain what had happened and provide evidence of the violation, but it was my role as the guild leader, and the worst was yet to come. Awards that were announced in the news were now taken from winners. I called an emergency board meeting to plan how we would handle the discipline of the members, since part of the group rules involved conduct that reflected on the guild.

My stomach was in knots. My nerves were raw. I hated signing certified letters to the members involved, knowing how I'd feel to receive one. Though the guild team expected enforcement of the rules and supported me, I wondered if I'd face a lawsuit because of someone's injured pride. I couldn't envision what the next guild meeting would look like, or who might take sides. I struggled not to let my imagination run to the worst scenarios and turned that energy toward prayer for wisdom, discernment, healing for damaged relationships, and the best outcome for all concerned.

As all this was happening, a contest winner in another national art magazine was disqualified for copying a journalist's photograph. A popular artist on the West Coast lost his highly publicized award, and like the previous national winner, he had to shut down his website over the controversy. I was keeping documentation of the drama in the two magazines and felt it was important to educate our guild members about what had happened on a national level. We devoted meetings to the topic and designed a brochure to answer the most basic questions.

For writers, textile artists, sculptors, artists, and crafters, be mindful of using copyrighted material and designs when you follow your creative muse. If you plan to enter competitions for awards or profit from your books, inspiration should be your own, not borrowed from someone else.

There are other areas of ethical concern if you plan to follow your creative calling as a business. Check your state laws for turning in sales taxes if you sell a product and talk to your tax professional about how to turn in your expenses and income.

If you plan to market your work, settle on a budget. Advertising is a daunting endeavor, and trends change every few months. To be honest, I loathe marketing and promotion, yet I can't avoid it. My health has suffered from stress and I sometimes long for the way my life was before I became a published author. Before you make a commitment, do your research about branding, promoting, creating websites, and all the other ins and outs of becoming a hobby or business. There is advice everywhere you turn, and many people will pose as experts. Pray for guidance about what to follow. Then be patient. The last estimate I heard is that it can take about five years to become established.

When listing your work in the marketplace, plan to ask for reviews. Prepare spiritually for both good reactions and rejection. Keep a "Sunbeams" file of the rewarding things that happen along the way—sales, emails from collectors who say they are blessed by your work, and other forms of encouragement. On bad days, open the file.

I am no longer on social media, except for LinkedIn, my YouTube channel, BookBub, and a non-political profile elsewhere. I now use a newsletter mailing list for communication with those who want to hear from me. If you are trying to follow marketing advice about an online social presence, you may want to set up a separate profile to keep your personal posts private. If you try the social media route for marketing, it will help to learn from other similar crafters. Practice how to talk about your creativity in public.

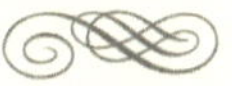

"Finally, brothers, whatever is true, whatever is honorable, whatever is just, whatever is pure, whatever is lovely, whatever is commendable—if there is any moral excellence and if there is any praise—dwell on these things."
Philippians 4:8

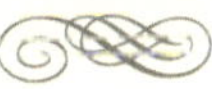

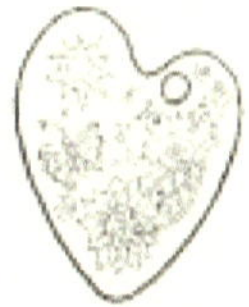

"YOUR WORD IS A LAMP for my feet and a light on my path." Psalm 119:105

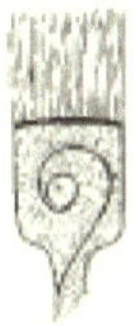

IN PSALM 1:1-3, A HAPPY man is described as one who doesn't follow bad advice. Instead, his delight is in the Lord. He is like a flourishing tree planted beside streams of water. Can this apply to Christians who practice their creative calling in the marketplace? Explain your answer.

AS AMBASSADORS FOR Christ, we should respect and follow the rules of all the settings we find ourselves in.

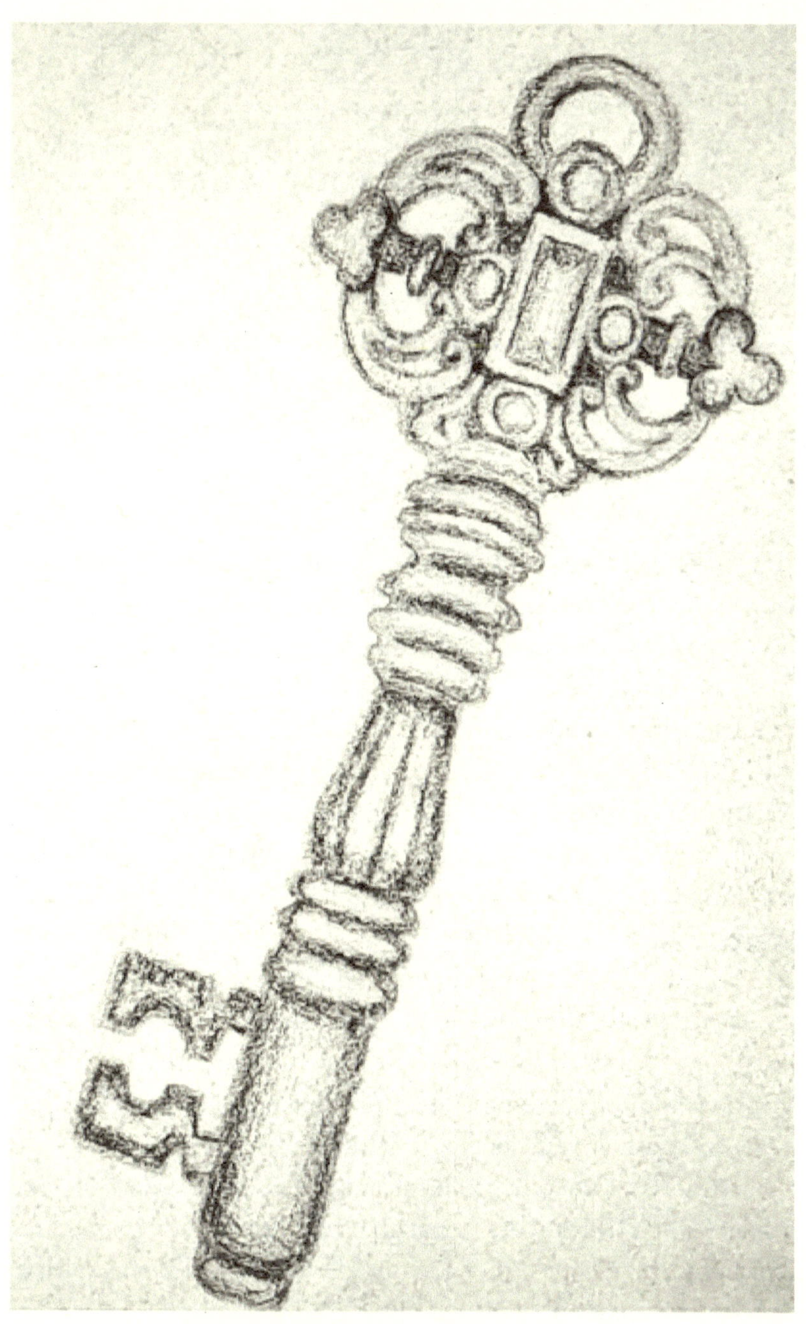

"Ancient Key"

The Value of Your Work

"I will buy them from you at full price. I won't offer to the Lord my God burnt offerings that cost me nothing."
2 Samuel 24:24

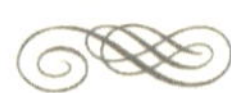

THE BIBLICAL ACCOUNT in 2 Samuel 24:18-24 is about Israel's King David purchasing highly situated land to build an altar. It's a story full of historical information about that site, agricultural information about threshing, and the rules for conducting offerings to Israel's God. It's unclear if the Jebusite landowner, as a foreigner, was sincere about giving the King the land or if he expected to get an offer for it.

The gist of the passage is what all the sermons I've heard about it have focused on—David knew that an offering was a sacrifice. It should cost him something. And God was pleased with it. He granted David's prayers to avert a calamity upon Israel.

I hope I've already communicated in this devotional that while the gift of creativity is a blessing, sharing it with the world will cost you something. That's as it should be. The pages of Scripture show how lavish God is with His blessings, but it also illustrates how the Holy Spirit in you will clash with the demonic spirit of the earth.

In a world of shattered feelings and unmet expectations, it's extraordinary when Christ works through us to create beauty that ignites a pilot light to someone's soul. But our efforts to provide this spirit-led healing balm comes at a precious price.

I've forgotten where I saw this statement or who said it, but a well-known man said his work as a thinker/philosopher/communicator took a lot of brainstorming, meditation, and time; yet no one these days will pay for that. The world pushes and pulls us, robbing us of introspection. The devices we created to free up our time have enslaved us. Under the bondage of technology, we are expected to produce the work of ten employees.

Creative Christians often feel guilty about finding time to pursue their giftedness and skills, and the stress of life builds when they have no outlet. A young artist I know works hard at a full-time job by day and tries to carve out time to paint at night. She once asked me about how to deal with people who wanted her to just give them her paintings.

Since I've grappled with this for years when asked to donate my time and resources to create art for good causes, I was ready with an answer she already knew was right: her time and vision have value. Unless she felt led to create and give away the painting, she shouldn't.

Creative Christians can be perceived as arrogant and uncaring when refusing to take on a task for free to help someone out, and often, we feel guilty. I have some "volunteer of the year" awards in my young adult past, and while it's something interesting if I had a scrapbook, I look back and know my family needed me more. A glance around at our younger generation is proof that many of us forgot that our first ministry is our spouse, children, and our home, and that role will demand all the creativity we can muster!

There will always be good causes and needy people, so we *must* be prayerful and discerning about boundaries on requests and expectations for free use of our time and talents. I encourage you to read the book of Nehemiah in the Bible and watch how he stayed the course of his calling rather than falling for the distractions that Satan sent his way.

Jesus is peace. He will never lead us to a state of chaos and over-commitment, which is worldly and from His enemy. Learn to say NO, because if you are exhausted and stressed out, *you are not in His will.*

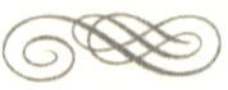

Stress is a joy stealer and a creativity killer.

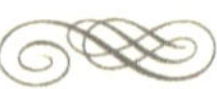

WHEN THE MOVIE DIVERGENT came out, I felt understood through the character of Tris. Finally, someone had written a story about how utterly crucial the creative, intuitive people in society are to the well-being of the whole. Despite the ease in which they are misunderstood and judged to be non-conformists; the world desperately needs them.

Creative people believe anything is possible, imagining the unimaginable and convinced it can be accomplished. Even if the goal is a long shot, they're willing to take risks and are the first to jump in and get to work, ignoring the naysayers whose voices have become a background buzz that's plagued and discouraged them all their lives. For Christians who embrace a God-given creative calling, life is brighter, ablaze with color, alive with movement, scents, tastes, and unusual sounds, and composed of intriguing shapes. Their senses pick up more information because they take time to look. In their eyes, the world is not a blur—it is loaded with meaning and possibilities!

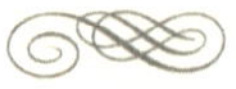

Set priorities and boundaries. More than most people, creative spirits need downtime to brainstorm and puzzle over inspiration. They are easily depleted by social interactions because they "spend" themselves lavishly on creativity.

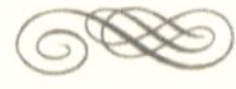

JUST THIS MORNING, I listened to a Christian author on her live video to readers and knew what she meant about having spent too much time around people over the weekend. She is an introvert whose love tank is full after being with friends and family at a birthday celebration, and now that she's home, she needs to recharge before getting back to her writing and research.

It helps us feel validated to hear people admit their limitations, doesn't it? As an introvert myself, I understood when she said that being with people drained her energy.

Let's look at another aspect in our stewardship of time and valuing our work. Are you competitive? If you are entering contests with your creative projects or comparing your work with what's on exhibition or the marketplace, it may be discouraging to see so many others being successful at their chosen crafts. I was blessed to be in a neighborhood craft group a few years ago, and most of our handmade creations are for ourselves, gifts, bartering among ourselves, and charities. Admiring the work of others is a gentle way to learn how we can improve, and that's necessary in growing our skills. But with that growth process comes the challenge not to envy the success of other people.

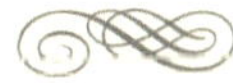

"WHENEVER YOU ATTEMPT a good work, you will find other men doing the same kind of work, and probably doing it better. Envy them not."

Henry Drummond, in *The Greatest Thing in the World,* 1884

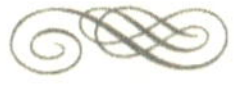

AS THIS BOOK ENDS, I want to share my thoughts about confidence and humility. This is a tricky balance, isn't it? We've established that creativity is a birthmark from our Creator, which makes it valuable. When we embrace creativity as a calling, our confidence is built on assurance. We abide in Christ. We follow the Spirit's lead, learning the skills it takes to become better at our craft. Our confidence builds as we compare our work with standards and evaluate it realistically. Doors of opportunity may open for us.

Even if we feel awkward about awards, accolades, applause, and recognition, we should allow people to express their appreciation of the blessing they received. Remember how you feel when you want to thank someone, and you'll know it's not about placing the person on an unrealistic pedestal. Encouragement from our audience is confirmation of our obedience to the Spirit's leadership.

Accepting appreciation is not a departure from humility. Godly humility is seeing reality and realizing that the Creator of the universe is the standard measure for everything else. It involves obedience to God's will and takes inner strength and confidence in His assurance of who we are to Him.

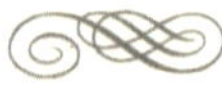

"Now to Him who is able to do above and beyond all that we ask or think according to the power that works in us— to Him be glory in the church and in Christ Jesus to all generations, forever and ever. Amen."
Ephesians 3:20-21

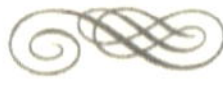

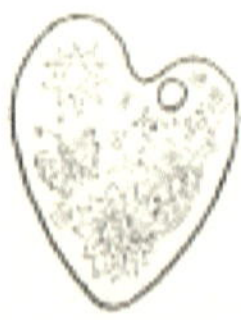

"BUT THE LORD IS FAITHFUL; He will strengthen and guard you from the evil one." 2 Thessalonians 3:3

"For the Lord watches over the way of the righteous..." Psalm 1:6

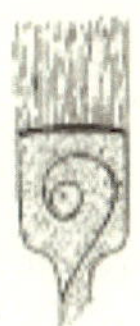

ROBERT LOUIS STEVENSON once said not to judge the day by the harvest we reap but by the seeds we plant. Are you planting seeds of simplicity and peace in your schedule to allow needed time for the communion you feel with Christ in your favorite expression of creativity?

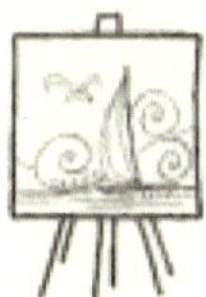

YOUR CREATIVE PURSUIT has the value you place on it. Set priorities with consideration to your responsibilities and relationships. If you find yourself longing for more creative time but have obligations that can't be changed, remember that this is only one season in your life. Keep the situation in prayer. In the meantime, appreciate the beauty, light, color, sounds, scents, and tastes all around you!

A Christian Artist's Prayer

Lord Jesus Christ our God, I come to You with a grateful heart for the evidence of Your divine hand as the Creator of all that exists. I'm filled with wonder and awe to know that I, too, am proof of Your majesty, for I bear the imprint of my Maker. Open my eyes, my soul, and my mind to experience the life You intended when You created me; grant me grace to overcome my tendency to stray from that walk with You.

My words aren't lofty, but heartfelt. I pray for Your Holy Spirit to fill my vision and guide my abilities. If it brings You glory, ignite my inspiration to touch the edges of fathomless mysteries in creation and the human soul. Grant me Spirit-filled expression to reach out as an ambassador for the Kingdom to come. As my Savior, I pray You will keep my heart clean and rule over my mind so that my creative endeavors are acceptable offerings that bear Your mark. If my work can open doors for the Gospel or be a blessing for fellow Christian believers, I pray for the confidence to step through and listen for Your guidance.

I pray also for my sisters and brothers in the faith who live out Your mandate in bearing the stamp of creativity. Grant us vibrant faith and Holy wisdom as we sprinkle salt and light in this world. Be the lamp that lights our path; divert us from discouragement and defeat. In our spiritual struggles and creative burnout, help us climb to the new level of skill You intend for us. Reveal Yourself to us in a fresh way and rekindle our passion for expressing Your glory to a world that desperately needs to see it. Amen.

To the Reader

Did you like this book? Please take a minute to recommend it to your friends and write a short review on your favorite book review sites. The author really appreciates it, and you will be doing the reading community a great service to help them find the books that appeal to them.

You can visit my websites to purchase books, stay updated with my blogs, enjoy free painting demos, free coloring pages, and newsletters!

Connect with Pamela Poole:

YouTube Channel: Pamela Poole, Artist and Author[1]

Artist Website: Pamela Poole Fine Art[2]

Publisher Website: Southern Sky Publishing[3]

1. *https://www.youtube.com/user/PamelaPooleFineArt*
2. *http://www.pamelapoole.com*
3. *http://www.southernskypublishing.com*

Becoming a Disciple of Jesus Christ

As you've been reading this devotional, have you realized there is much more to living as a Christian believer than you've experienced? Jesus lived a sinless life, but He died in our place as if He was the guilty one. Who is Jesus to you? Do you know Him, and if not, do you want to?

If you're serious about knowing Jesus and committing to the next steps to become more mature in your faith, talk to a trusted fellow Christian friend or pastor. Perhaps you don't have a church family. In that case, there are many straightforward resources online to find answers and assurances to questions you have. Here is a simple page link at Got Questions.

https://www.gotquestions.org/become-a-Christian.html

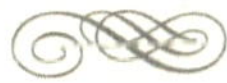

Once you've decided to entrust your salvation to Jesus, it's important that you get involved in a doctrinally solid local church to begin your walk as a disciple. Prayerfully seek the Lord's guidance to help you find that church home.

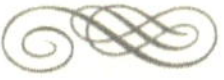

"Jesus told him, 'I am the way, the truth, and the life. No one comes to the Father except through Me.'"
John 14:6

About the Author

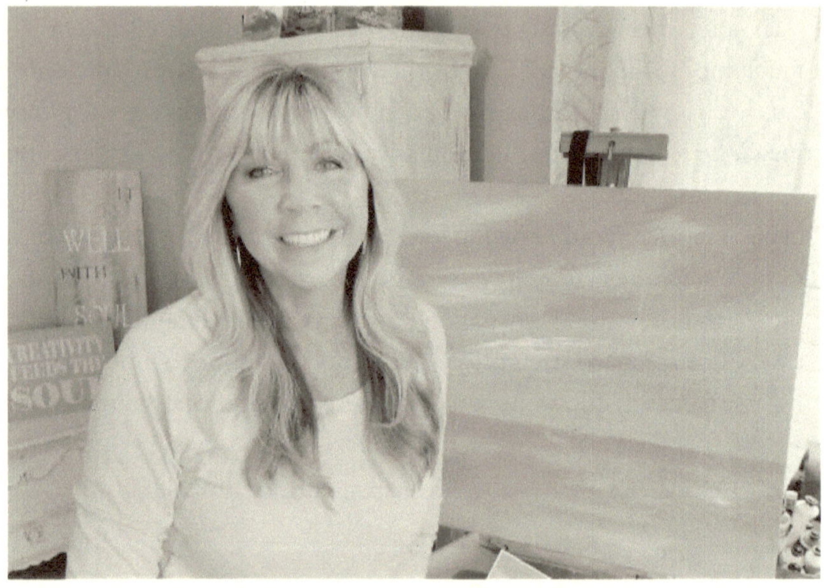

Pamela Poole's love for the South inspires all her books and paintings. It's why she describes her work as "Southern Ambiance." She and her husband Mark live in the Low Country of South Carolina.

Her perspective on writing books and painting is like that of the iconic artist Norman Rockwell, who once said he knew life was not ideal, but it should be, so he chose to paint that way. Pamela has experienced enough "reality" in life and pursues the warm, whimsical, loving, and ideal in her creativity. She hopes readers will laugh out loud, sigh, be inspired to reach higher, and feel refreshed, as if they've been for a walk in warm Southern sunshine!

Pamela writes clean fiction from a Christian worldview, but she was an artist before she became an author. Her stories often feature artists and art perspectives that help any reader have a deeper appreciation for painting.

Pamela lives life loving Jesus and her family as a wife, mother, and Gigi, and she is blessed with true friends.

"Now to Him who is able to do above and beyond all that we ask or think according to the power that works in us— to Him be glory in the church and in Christ Jesus to all generations, forever and ever. Amen." Ephesians 3:20,21

FREE BOOK DOWNLOAD!

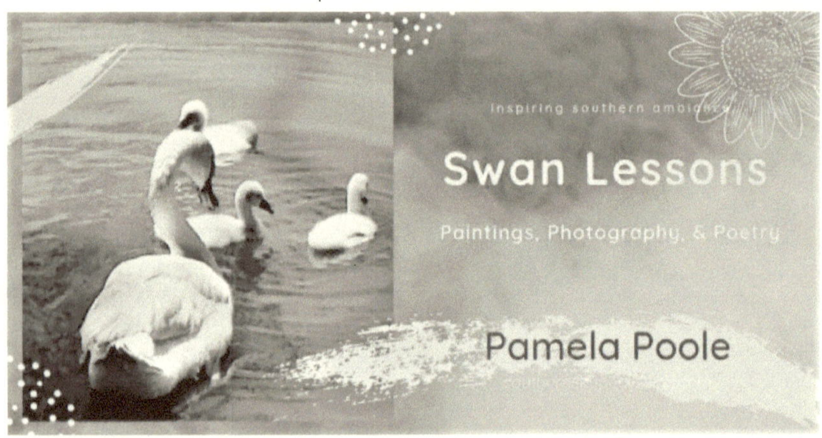

For a FREE DOWNLOAD of ***Swan Lessons–Painting, Photography, and Poetry*** go to the Home Page of Southern Sky Publishing. Look for the photo and button beside the *Southern Sky Publishing* title under the slide show. No sign-ups or gimmicks! I designed this gift to share with those who appreciate nature, art, and creative poetry, so let your friends know about the link. The inspiration for the booklet is a swan couple that lived in the small lake in my backyard at the last home we lived in. They have reminded me of life truths that became short poems, and their calm grace, elegance, and beauty inspired my paintings and nature photography. I hope it will be a blessing to you!

Swan Lessons—Painting, Photography, and Poetry
Southern Sky Publishing
www.southernskypublishing.com

Books in the Painter Place Saga

The Painter Place Saga is about the lives of an artistic Christian family.

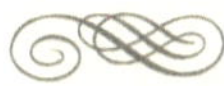

Novels

Painter Place, Painter Place Saga 1

Hugo, Painter Place Saga 2

Jaguar, Painter Place Saga 3

Landmark, Painter Place Saga 4

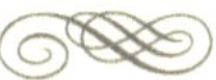

Legends (Short Stories)

The Wind Song of the Marsh, Legend 1

King's Ransom, Legend 2

The Castaway and the Mermaid, Legend 3

The Strange Sands Suspense Series

The Old Cedar Chest
The Hidden Hallway
The Freedom Staircase
The Dark Passage
The Devil's Drawer (coming soon!)

Landmark, Painter Place Saga 4

The Painter Place Saga is filled with life lessons and insights related to the lives of working artists who are Christians. In this excerpt from the newest release in the series, Wyeth Painter finds that his intention for a painting is diverted when he joins Christ in what He's doing in the life of a guest on the island.

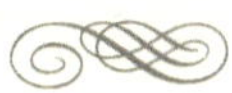

WYETH TRIED PAINTING the marsh view from the new windows in his studio, but the portrait of Chrissy lurked behind him as surely as her father had on the yacht last Friday night. Finally, he stood and stretched, satisfied with the blocking-in stage of the landscape he was working on.

I can put the portrait in storage for now, he thought. But he didn't. Ignoring it, he went to get his outdoor painting gear ready.

His dad came to the open studio door. "I wondered why I heard you packin' up instead of painting. Can't get the view through the windows?"

Wyeth glanced up. "Oh, yeah, I got a great start on a large landscape. I need to get outside that's all."

He felt his dad watching him. "Want a tag-a-long?"

"Oh, thanks, but I know you're tryin' to finish up the painting for the show in Charlotte. I may go out to the chapel. We sold the last painting in inventory. Can I use your truck?"

His dad stepped back from the door to let him pass into the hall, commenting that they couldn't seem to keep paintings of the chapel in stock. Then he dug into his pocket for keys. When he put them in Wyeth's hand, he held on to it.

Wyeth had to look away from the searching scrutiny in his father's wise, sea-blue eyes, but he didn't pull his hand away. Quietly, he told him, "I can't talk about it now, Dad."

With a nod and a firm pat on Wyeth's hand, his dad said brightly, "You're twenty-two years old, son. It's time you stopped borrowin' my truck. Let's go look for a car soon."

Relieved, Wyeth answered, "Yeah, I need to decide on one. We'll go drive a few on your next day off."

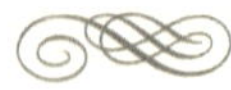

A GUEST WAS IN THE Painter chapel when Wyeth pulled the truck into a sandy parking area nearby. A bicycle leaned on its kickstand near a short column where a weathered verdigris sundial rested, and he recognized the sea-glass green paint color as the code belonging to one of the island cottages. He tried not to disturb anyone inside while he selected a view of the building and set up his easel under a shady grove of palm trees.

He pulled out a small canvas hoping he could finish in one session, making sure the back was stamped with the Painter Gallery branding. The new acrylic paints made it easy to have a day's work dry and ready to hang in the island gallery.

There was a new technique he wanted to experiment with, using transparent layering to achieve a sunlit glow on the side of the building. But it was a slower process than he expected. After several times when he caught himself clenching his jaw in impatience, he stepped away to the truck and grabbed a thermos of cold water.

He leaned back against the door and stared at the chapel, searching for some key he missed that would help the painting. After several gulps of water, he looked away, into the garden.

Why was he so frustrated with a painting? If it didn't work out, he'd paint over it. It was no big deal. Yet he made a big deal out of everything these days as if he wore a "Do Not Disturb" sign to warn life to leave him alone. He was unsure which was worse, to grapple with life's challenges in fear of making a mistake or to have nothing special ever happen to him.

He put the thermos back on the front seat of his dad's truck and shut the door. With a purpose in his stride, he went to stand in front of the easel, refreshed his palette, and painted again. As he painted, he poured out his heart in prayer, as the person in the chapel was doing. By the time he finished, the guest came out the double front doors.

Upon noticing Wyeth, a young lady wiped her eyes and re-did her auburn ponytail. She went to the bicycle but didn't get on to ride. Instead, she looked back at him and then at the chapel.

Wyeth stopped short of a groan under his breath and waved back at her politely. Now, he was stuck talking about the painting, and maybe about the whole island once she asked him who he was. His stomach was growling for the late lunch he knew Maggie Jane was keeping for him.

The young lady walked the bike over to his easel. "Excuse me, sir, but are you painting the chapel?"

"Yes, ma'am. Nice day for a bike ride. Hope you're enjoyin' the island."

"Oh, yes, it is, and I am. I'm here with my aunt, as a companion to help her this summer. She's a writer. We leave tomorrow, so I asked for the afternoon to roam around. May I see your painting?"

Wyeth stepped back. "Sure."

The young lady pushed down the kickstand on the bike and came over to look at the picture. Then, she brought her hands to her mouth. After a few moments she asked, "Is that what it looked like out here while I was praying?"

"I'll never be able to capture it the way it really was."

"I knew it! At first, I pleaded for what I want, for a sign, or something Jesus could do to help me make the right decision. After so long in the chapel, feeling like my prayers were only hanging out around me, I told Him I'd go His way, if I could only see it. After a while, I didn't know what else to say to Him except that I love and trust Him, whatever the outcome. He hears us, I know that by faith. But it didn't feel like He was there."

Her ponytail swished as she turned to Wyeth. "He was out here, with you!"

Wyeth stared at the painting to see how she'd come up with that idea, then he looked up at the building. The light had already changed. "Ma'am, Christ is omniscient and omnipresent. He's with you and me at the same time."

"Were you praying, too?"

His expression was her answer. "Yes, you were. What did you pray for?"

Wyeth shifted his weight to the other leg. "The same thing. It's a universal condition, what we're seeking. In the end, even if we don't get what we want, we trust in the right outcome. Some of the most solid people I know are the ones who had bad outcomes and grew from the experience."

She looked back at the painting and whispered, "He was here. His presence is so clear in this painting."

"Would you like to have it?"

"Oh, yes! Is it for sale?"

"No, ma'am, but I'll give it to you. In dark times, maybe it will help you remember that Christ is always with those who love and follow Him."

Acknowledgements

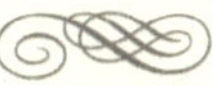

This devotional took me far out of my comfort zone! There must be a purpose for looking back over the artistic landmarks in my life and re-living experiences that made my faith grow. Everything I write is for an audience of myself and Jesus, and I know this book will help me remember who I am in Him when trials come. I'm so blessed by the prayers of friends and family and I appreciate the special support I had for this project from Cheryl Coleman, J.E. Grace, and Karen Summey.

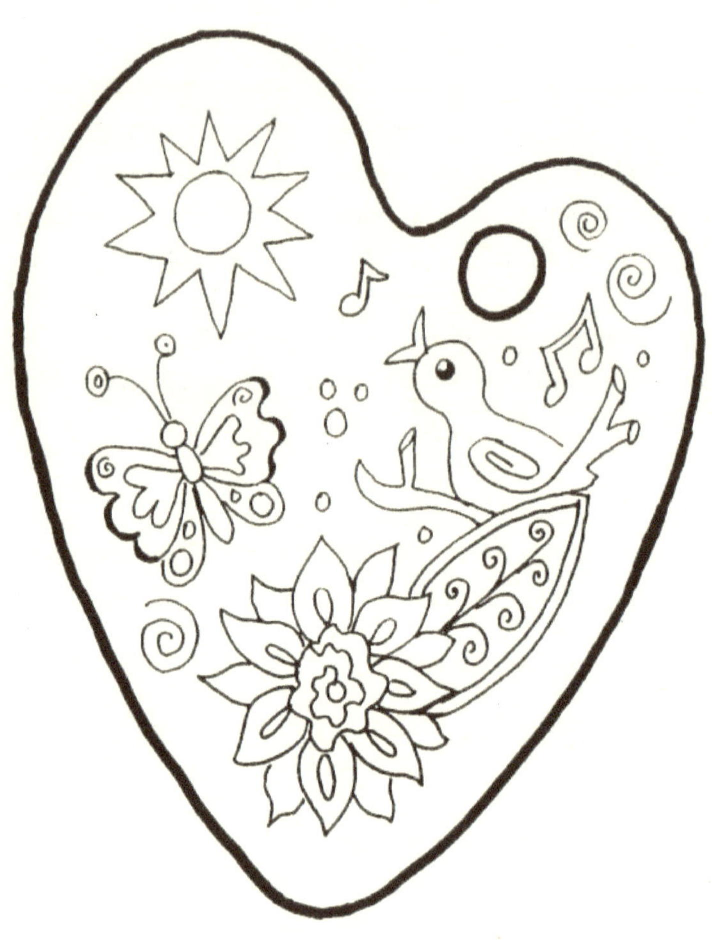

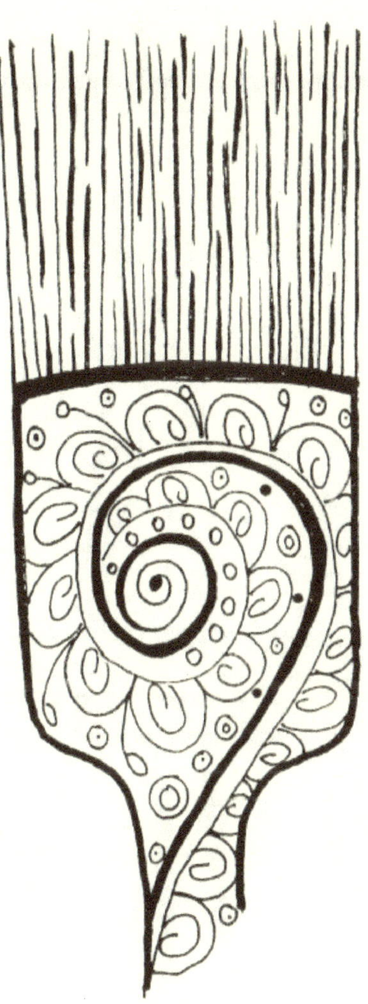

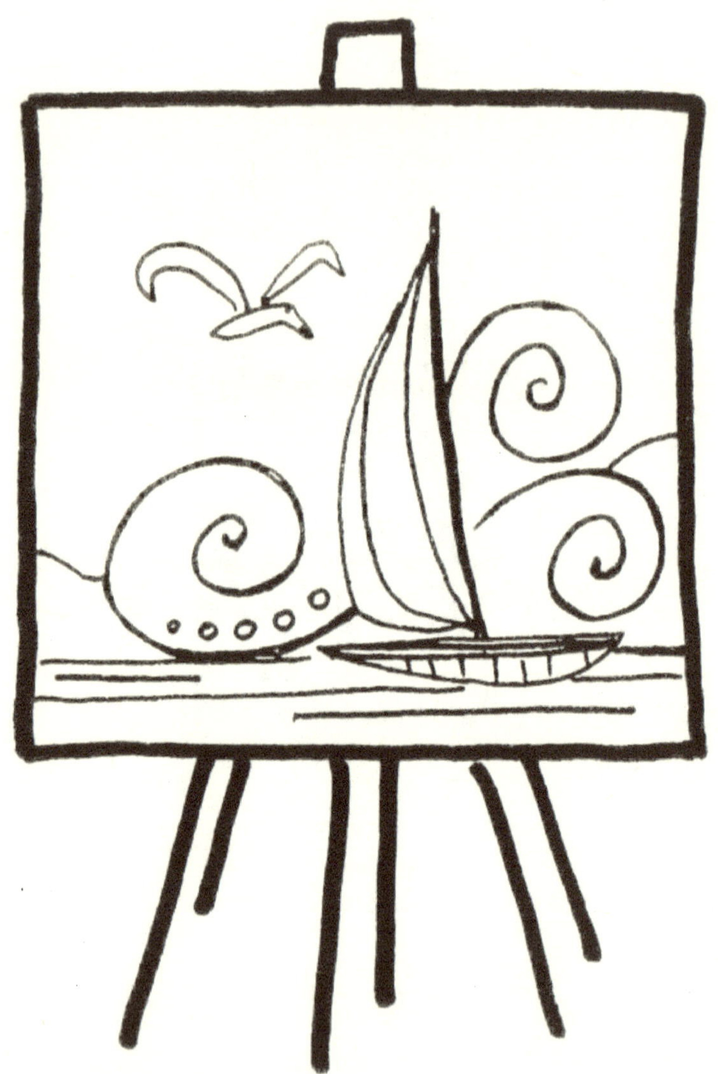

Inspired Musings

These extra pages in the back of the print version of the devotional are for the reader's personal notes. Fill them with your inspiration and thoughts or the answers to the questions at the end of each chapter.

Inspired Musings

Which scripture verses and passages speak about what inspires you?

Inspired Musings

What gift of creative inspiration will you act on in the future? What challenges will this bring?

www.ingramcontent.com/pod-product-compliance
Lightning Source LLC
LaVergne TN
LVHW050935080826
845145LV00004B/1277

* 9 7 8 1 9 5 6 0 8 9 1 0 3 *